WINDOWS ON THE WORLD

THE BODY
AND HOW IT WORKS

Written by
Steve Parker

Illustrated by
Giovanni Caselli
Guiliano Fornari
Sergio

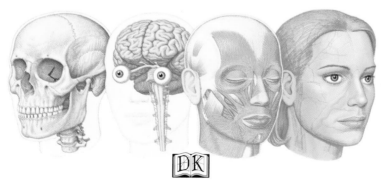

DK

DORLING KINDERSLEY
London • New York • Moscow • Sydney

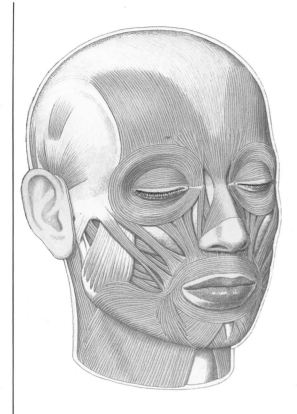

[DK]

A Dorling Kindersley Book

Editor Angela Wilkes
Art editor Roger Priddy

Editorial director Jackie Douglas
Art director Roger Bristow

Editorial consultant Dr. Frances Williams

Published in Great Britain by
Dorling Kindersley Limited,
9 Henrietta Street, London WC2E 8PS

Paperback edition
2 4 6 8 10 9 7 5 3 1

Copyright © 1987, 1998 Dorling Kindersley
Limited, London

Visit us on the World Wide Web at:
http://www.dk.com.

A CIP catalogue record for this book is available
from the British Library.

ISBN: 0-7513-5735-9

Reproduced in Singapore by Colourscan
Printed and bound in Spain by Artes Gráficas Toledo, S.A.
D.L. TO: 42-1998

CONTENTS

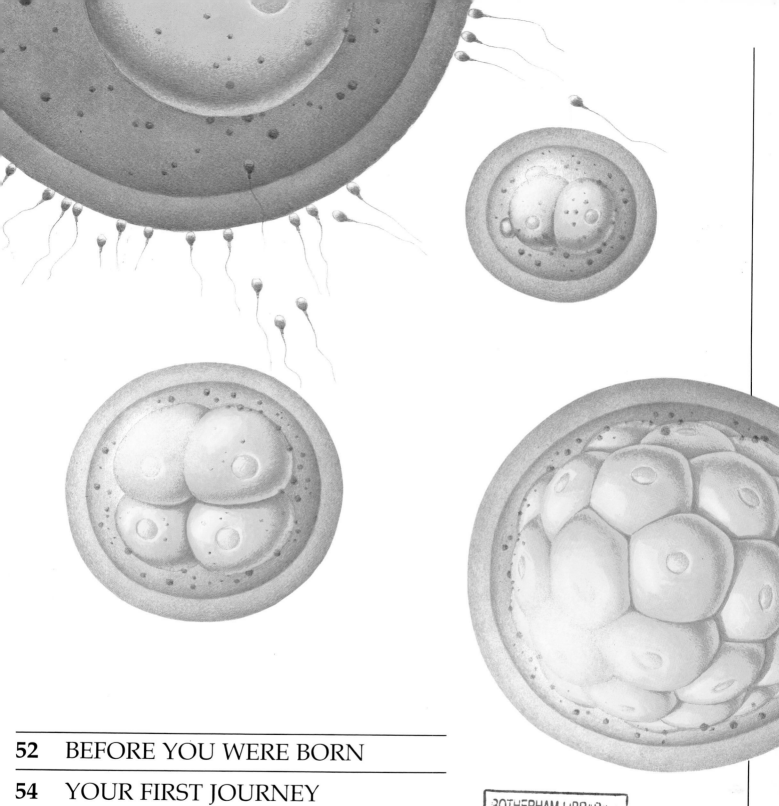

THE BODY MACHINE

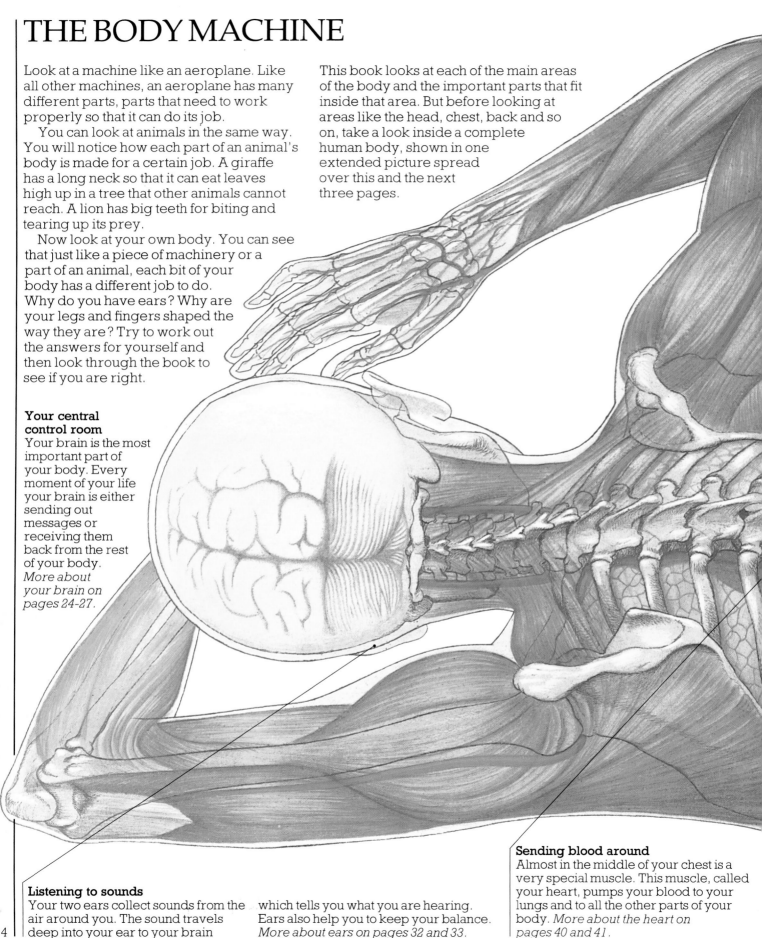

Look at a machine like an aeroplane. Like all other machines, an aeroplane has many different parts, parts that need to work properly so that it can do its job.

You can look at animals in the same way. You will notice how each part of an animal's body is made for a certain job. A giraffe has a long neck so that it can eat leaves high up in a tree that other animals cannot reach. A lion has big teeth for biting and tearing up its prey.

Now look at your own body. You can see that just like a piece of machinery or a part of an animal, each bit of your body has a different job to do. Why do you have ears? Why are your legs and fingers shaped the way they are? Try to work out the answers for yourself and then look through the book to see if you are right.

This book looks at each of the main areas of the body and the important parts that fit inside that area. But before looking at areas like the head, chest, back and so on, take a look inside a complete human body, shown in one extended picture spread over this and the next three pages.

Your central control room

Your brain is the most important part of your body. Every moment of your life your brain is either sending out messages or receiving them back from the rest of your body. *More about your brain on pages 24-27.*

Listening to sounds

Your two ears collect sounds from the air around you. The sound travels deep into your ear to your brain which tells you what you are hearing. Ears also help you to keep your balance. *More about ears on pages 32 and 33.*

Sending blood around

Almost in the middle of your chest is a very special muscle. This muscle, called your heart, pumps your blood to your lungs and to all the other parts of your body. *More about the heart on pages 40 and 41.*

Holding on to things

Your arm is like a pole attached to your hand so that you can reach out. Your hand is a most useful part of your body. It is made up of a flat palm, four fingers and a thumb. By bending your fingers or holding them against your palm, you can grasp objects, use tools, push things away or pull things towards you. *More on arms and hands on pages 42 and 43.*

Your body's transport system

The red liquid that flows around your body is blood. Blood is very important because it carries food and oxygen from one part of your body to another. Your heart pumps your blood through your body along tubes called arteries. Blood travels back to your heart through narrower tubes called veins. *More about blood on pages 16 and 17.*

Breathing in air

A lot of space inside your chest is taken up by two spongy bags called lungs. When you breathe in, air goes down into your lungs so that they fill up like balloons. Some of the air goes to other parts of your body. What's left is pushed out of your lungs when you breathe out. *More about lungs on pages 38 and 39.*

What's inside your body?

The picture below of the back of a person's body shows how well designed the human body is. Many parts of the body are delicate, so the most important parts are protected by strong bones. The brain, the body's control centre, is protected by the skull. Bones in the back and chest protect the heart that pumps your blood and the lungs you need for breathing. The hip bone protects other important parts.

Your body's framework

All the hard parts inside your body are bones. You have about 200 bones in your body, and when they all fit together they make up your skeleton. Bones not only give your body a strong frame, they also protect your insides and allow you to move. *More about bones on pages 18-21.*

How food leaves your body

After food leaves your stomach, it travels on through a long tube called your intestine. Here some food is taken into your body to be used to make you grow or to give you energy. Any food still left by the time it reaches the end of the tube, leaves your body as waste. *More about your digestive system on pages 46 to 49.*

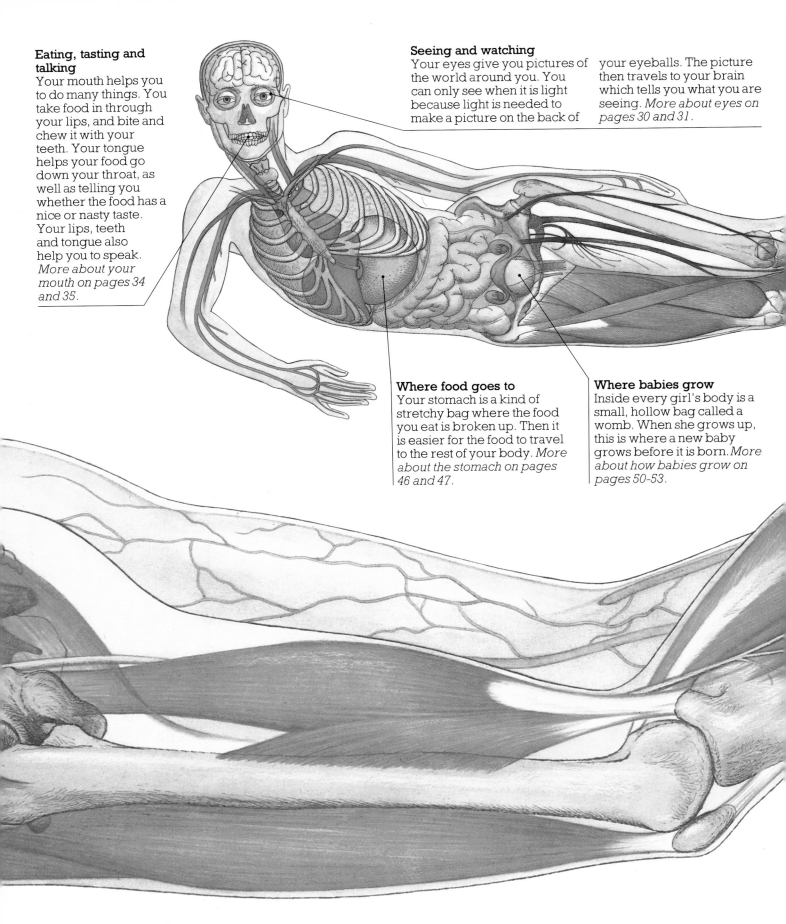

Eating, tasting and talking

Your mouth helps you to do many things. You take food in through your lips, and bite and chew it with your teeth. Your tongue helps your food go down your throat, as well as telling you whether the food has a nice or nasty taste. Your lips, teeth and tongue also help you to speak. *More about your mouth on pages 34 and 35.*

Seeing and watching

Your eyes give you pictures of the world around you. You can only see when it is light because light is needed to make a picture on the back of your eyeballs. The picture then travels to your brain which tells you what you are seeing. *More about eyes on pages 30 and 31.*

Where food goes to

Your stomach is a kind of stretchy bag where the food you eat is broken up. Then it is easier for the food to travel to the rest of your body. *More about the stomach on pages 46 and 47.*

Where babies grow

Inside every girl's body is a small, hollow bag called a womb. When she grows up, this is where a new baby grows before it is born. *More about how babies grow on pages 50-53.*

Inside the legs and feet

In the picture above you can see inside the lower part of a person's body.

The front of a girl's body
The picture on the left shows what the front of a girl's body would look like if you could see inside her. Many of the most important parts of the body can only be seen from the front.

Carrying messages around
In every part of your body you have tiny connecting "wires" called nerves. Some nerves carry messages to your brain telling it what the rest of your body is feeling. Other nerves take orders from your brain to your muscles, telling them when to move. *More about nerves on pages 12 and 13.*

A protective covering
The whole of your body is covered by skin. Skin not only helps to prevent your insides from being hurt or catching illnesses, it also keeps your body from getting too hot or too cold. *More about skin on pages 8-11.*

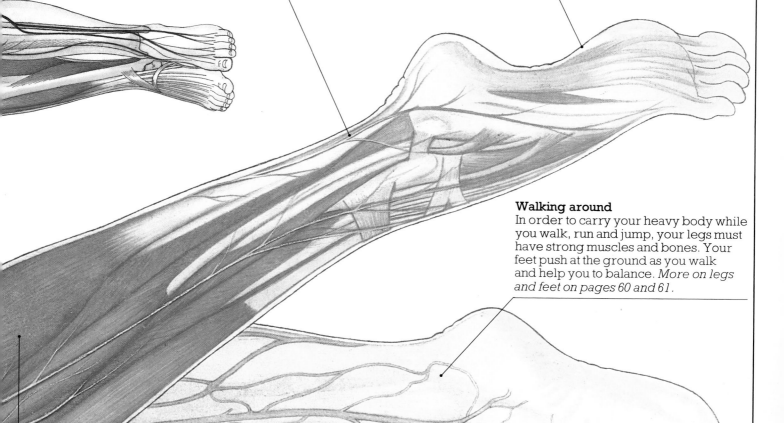

Walking around
In order to carry your heavy body while you walk, run and jump, your legs must have strong muscles and bones. Your feet push at the ground as you walk and help you to balance. *More on legs and feet on pages 60 and 61.*

Moving about
Muscles are the parts inside your body that make you move. They are joined to your bones. All muscles are under orders from your brain. When your brain tells them to work, they do so by pulling a bone or by bending or straightening a joint. *More about muscles on pages 14 and 15.*

Facts about your body

Your body contains
- 206 bones
- about 639 muscles

Of your total body weight
- your skin makes up more than 10%
- your muscles take up 40%
- your bones take up 25%
- your brain takes up 2%

Your heart beats
- an average of 70 times a minute
- 100,000 times a day without rest throughout your lifetime

When you were born you were probably
- about 28% of your final height if you are a boy
- about 30% of your final height if you are a girl

Your brain
- has 10 million nerve cells
- has a potential 25,000 interconnections with other nerve cells around your body
- is made up of 80% water

The whole of your body
- is about 70% water

YOUR SKIN

When you look at your body, the main part you can see is skin. It is your all-purpose covering. It is waterproof – in both directions. It keeps water out and, more important, it keeps water in. Your insides have to be kept moist and bathed in body fluids, or they would dry out and stop working. (In fact skin is more showerproof than waterproof, since if you stayed in water for too long your skin would go soggy and begin to leak.)

Skin is germ-proof. It is a tough barrier that keeps harmful microbes out of your body. Most germs get into the body through "gaps" in the skin, such as the nose and mouth, or through a cut in the skin. Skin also protects your insides from the sun's potentially harmful ultra-violet rays.

Skin is flexible and supple. As you move it stretches to cover the parts that bend, then it springs back into shape afterwards. So it always fits your body well!

Skin does not wear away. It is always replacing itself (*see page 10*). If it is rubbed harder, skin becomes even thicker, in order to resist the wear. This is why people who do heavy work with their hands have hard, thick (*callous*) patches of skin on them. If skin is damaged or cut, it is able to repair itself automatically.

Skin does many other jobs. It helps to keep your body at the right temperature and it has the sense of touch, as you can read on the following pages.

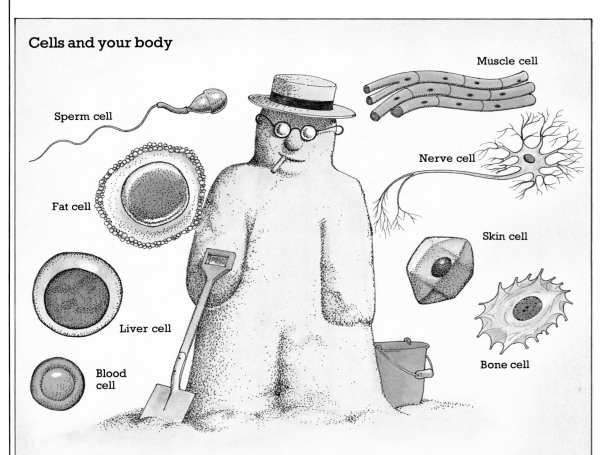

Cells and your body

Muscle cell

Sperm cell

Nerve cell

Fat cell

Skin cell

Liver cell

Bone cell

Blood cell

A sandman is made of tiny grains of sand. In a way, you are like a sandman. Your body is made of tiny parts too, called cells. In your case, however, not all these parts are the same. There are many different kinds of cell in various parts of your body. Some of them are shown above. Each main part, or *organ,* of your body is made of different kinds of cell. The shape of each cell depends on what job it does and cells are always doing their jobs, making chemicals, or changing one substance into another, or dividing to form new cells. Some cells, like those in your skin and blood, only live for a few weeks. Other cells, such as those in your nerves and bones, may be as old as you are. An average cell is about one-thirtieth of a millimetre across – so small that you can only see it with a microscope. There are about 50,000 million cells of different kinds in your body.

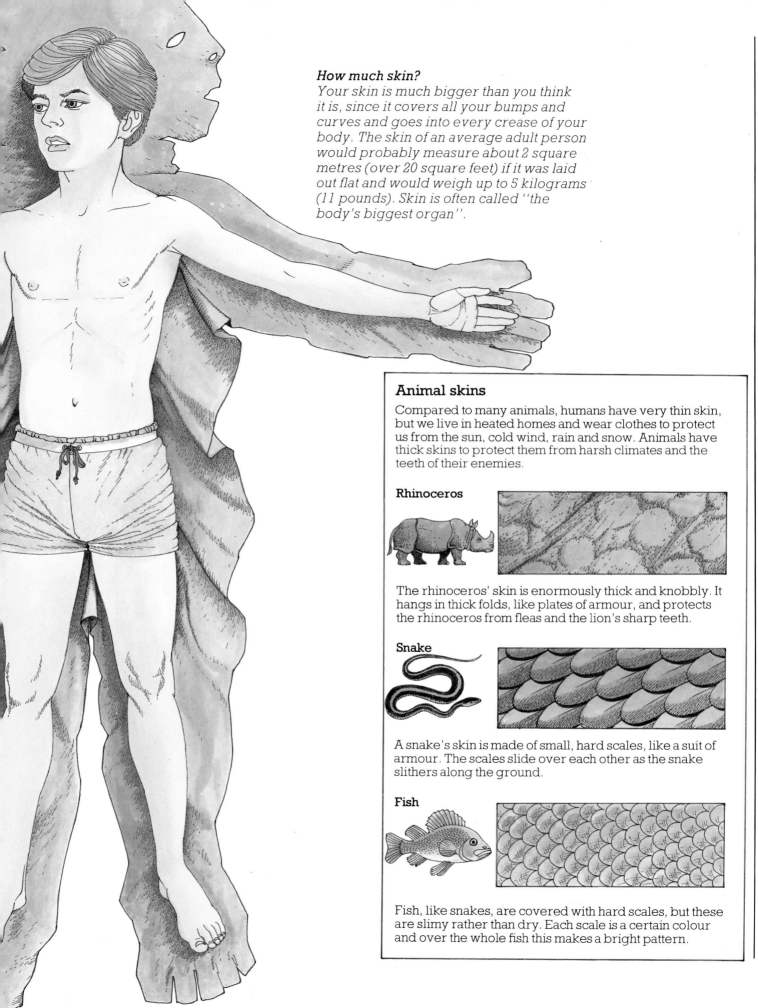

How much skin?

Your skin is much bigger than you think it is, since it covers all your bumps and curves and goes into every crease of your body. The skin of an average adult person would probably measure about 2 square metres (over 20 square feet) if it was laid out flat and would weigh up to 5 kilograms (11 pounds). Skin is often called "the body's biggest organ".

Animal skins

Compared to many animals, humans have very thin skin, but we live in heated homes and wear clothes to protect us from the sun, cold wind, rain and snow. Animals have thick skins to protect them from harsh climates and the teeth of their enemies.

Rhinoceros

The rhinoceros' skin is enormously thick and knobbly. It hangs in thick folds, like plates of armour, and protects the rhinoceros from fleas and the lion's sharp teeth.

Snake

A snake's skin is made of small, hard scales, like a suit of armour. The scales slide over each other as the snake slithers along the ground.

Fish

Fish, like snakes, are covered with hard scales, but these are slimy rather than dry. Each scale is a certain colour and over the whole fish this makes a bright pattern.

UNDER YOUR SKIN

On the outside, you are dead. Your hair and the surface of your skin are made of dead cells. But less than a millimetre under the surface of your skin are some of the busiest cells in your body. They are continually dividing to make new layers of skin cells which harden and die, to replace the top layer of skin as it is worn away. Every day millions of dead skin cells rub off as you have a wash, dry yourself with a towel, get dressed and move about. Much of the "dust" in a house is dead skin which has rubbed off people's bodies.

This wearing-away only happens in the top part of the skin, which is called the *epidermis.* The epidermis is designed to protect the lower layer of your skin, the *dermis.* The dermis is made of a tough, elastic substance that gives skin its stretchiness and springiness. In the dermis are the blood vessels that bring food to your skin ; the nerve endings that sense touch, heat, cold and pain ; and the sweat glands and oil glands that help to keep your skin supple and waterproof.

Your skin is not the same all over your body. On your hands it has lots of tiny ridges for a good grip. On the soles of your feet the skin is very thick, since this is where it wears away the most.

Inside skin
On most parts of your body your skin is about one millimetre thick. Under a microscope you can see the two main layers – the epidermis (the top, dark layer) and the dermis. This bit of skin comes from the top of your head, and the hairs look like giant tree trunks.

On the surface
The hard, dead cells on the surface of your skin lock together like tiles on a roof. As they wear away, more dead cells move up from below.

Making new skin
At the bottom of the epidermis, new skin cells are continuously being made. They slowly thicken, harden and die as they are pushed up by more new cells.

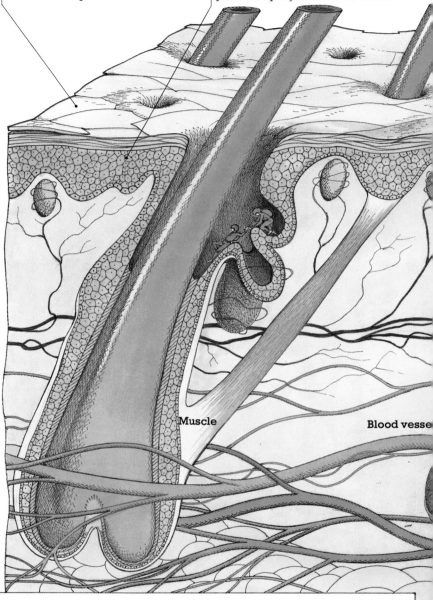

Muscle

Blood vesse

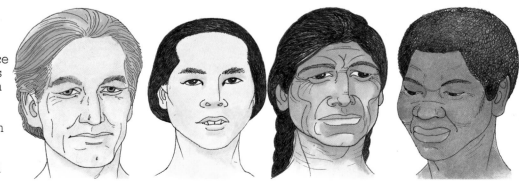

Colour is skin deep
People whose ancestors came from different parts of the world have different coloured skin. All skin contains a colouring substance called *melanin.* Dark skin contains more of it than fair skin, as melanin protects the skin from damage by too much sun by "shading" the deeper layers of skin. People from hot, sunny places have dark skin. Those from cooler places are fair-skinned because they do not need as much protection, but they get a tan if they spend a lot of time in the sun. Beneath the skin everyone is exactly the same.

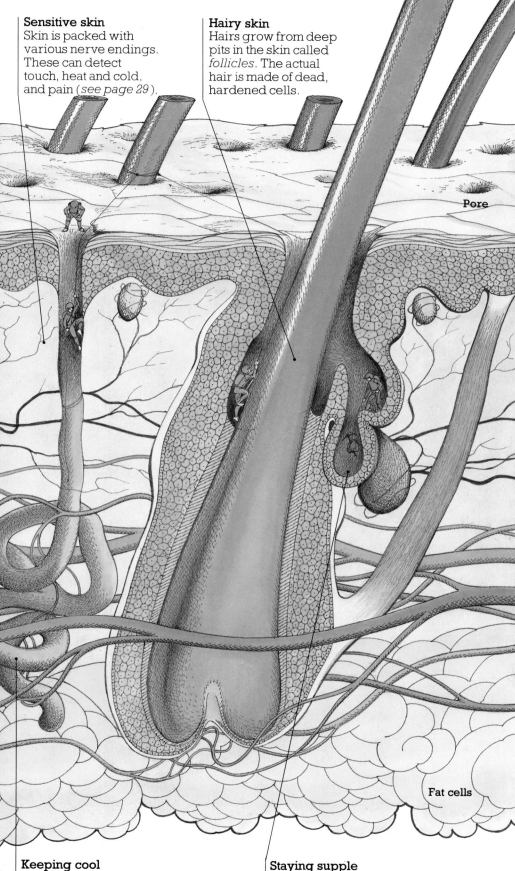

Sensitive skin
Skin is packed with various nerve endings. These can detect touch, heat and cold, and pain (*see page 29*).

Hairy skin
Hairs grow from deep pits in the skin called *follicles*. The actual hair is made of dead, hardened cells.

Pore

Fat cells

Keeping cool
Deep in the lower layer of skin are coiled-up tubes called sweat glands. You have about three million of them altogether. They make watery sweat that cools your body.

Staying supple
Waxy and oily substances are made by tiny glands (*sebaceous* glands) near each hair. These "natural oils" prevent your skin from drying out and cracking, and keep it soft and supple.

Temperature control
Your skin helps you to stay at your ideal temperature of 37°C. Your brain controls how much blood flows through your skin, to regulate your temperature.

Flushing

When you get too hot, the blood vessels in your skin become wider. More blood flows through them, so you lose more heat and cool down. The extra blood in your skin makes you look pink or "flushed".

Sweating

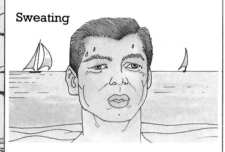

Another way of staying cool is by sweating. Watery sweat comes from the skin's sweat glands (see left). As the sweat evaporates, it draws heat from your body to cool it. You can help by splashing yourself with cold water.

Pale and shivering

When it's cold, the blood vessels in your skin become narrower. This cuts down the amount of heat lost through your skin, and makes you look pale. Your muscles help to make extra heat by working on their own – this is what we call "shivering".

YOUR NERVES

Your body is buzzing with electricity. Even when you are asleep, electrical signals are flashing to and fro, as one part of the body signals to another. The amounts of electricity in the signals are tiny, only a fraction of the strength of a telephone signal or even a torch battery. But they are strong enough to make your muscles work and to tell you about your surroundings, using your senses. These tiny signals are called nerve impulses.

The "wires" of the body are called nerves. They run in large bundles, like electrical cables, all over your body. Each nerve separates and connects to a certain part. Most nerves run to and from the brain, which is the "control centre" of the whole nervous system (*see page 24*).

Nerves are made of cells called *neurons*. A single nerve cell is much thinner than an ordinary electrical wire – it's about one-hundredth of a millimetre across. But, like a wire, it can be very long. The nerve cells that go right down to your toes might be over a metre long!

Sending signals

Your nervous system has connections to all the parts of your body. Part of the system runs automatically – keeping your lungs breathing, for instance. Other nerves go into action when you want to do something, such as clench your fist.

A tunnel of bone

Nerve cells are very delicate. Many types of cell can divide to form new cells if they are damaged, but a nerve cell cannot. So the body has to protect its nerves. Your brain is in a hard, bony box – your skull. Your spinal cord is in a flexible bony tunnel – your backbone, or spine. To connect to the body, nerves branch off from your spinal cord and run between the separate bones (*vertebrae*) of your backbone.

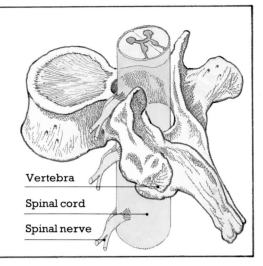

Vertebra

Spinal cord

Spinal nerve

Quicker than thinking

Many nerves connect to the brain, but they also connect directly to other nerves that make muscles move. In the "knee-jerk", a tap just below your knee makes your leg jump. This is a *reflex*, a "short-circuit", as it bypasses nerves which connect to the brain.

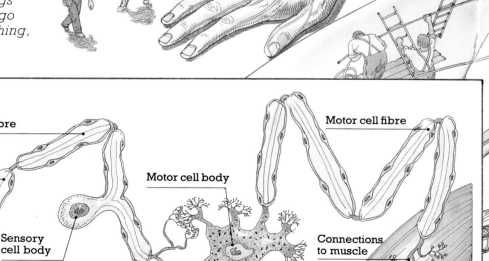

Passing on signals

Sensory cell fibre

Signals passing along nerve fibre

Motor cell fibre

Motor cell body

Sensory cell body

Tiny gaps between cells

Connections to muscle

Myelin sheath

Here is the simplest nerve connection imaginable: one sensory cell and one motor cell. Each of them has a fat cell body and a long, thin extension which is the nerve fibre. Like the plastic covering on a wire, the fibre has a fatty covering called the *myelin sheath*, which insulates it. When the sensory cell detects something it sends out lots of signals. They flash along the nerve fibre, protected by the myelin sheath, and jump a tiny gap to the motor cell. Carrying on, they reach the muscle and make it tighten.

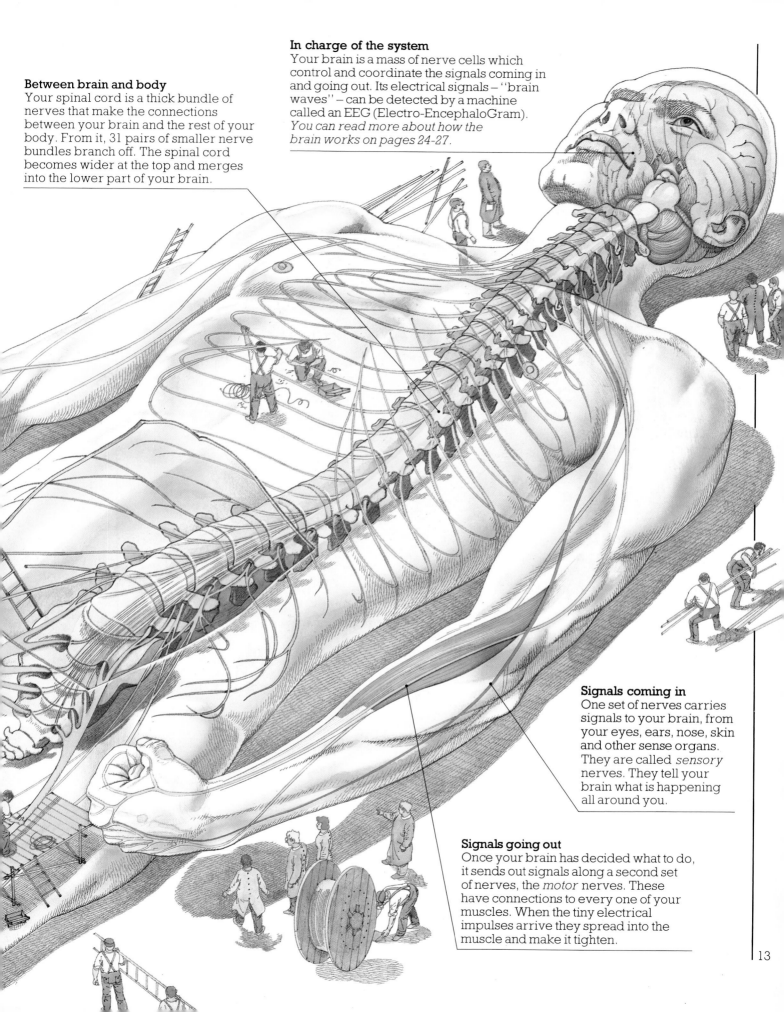

Between brain and body
Your spinal cord is a thick bundle of nerves that make the connections between your brain and the rest of your body. From it, 31 pairs of smaller nerve bundles branch off. The spinal cord becomes wider at the top and merges into the lower part of your brain.

In charge of the system
Your brain is a mass of nerve cells which control and coordinate the signals coming in and going out. Its electrical signals – "brain waves" – can be detected by a machine called an EEG (Electro-EncephaloGram). *You can read more about how the brain works on pages 24-27.*

Signals coming in
One set of nerves carries signals to your brain, from your eyes, ears, nose, skin and other sense organs. They are called *sensory* nerves. They tell your brain what is happening all around you.

Signals going out
Once your brain has decided what to do, it sends out signals along a second set of nerves, the *motor* nerves. These have connections to every one of your muscles. When the tiny electrical impulses arrive they spread into the muscle and make it tighten.

MUSCLES AND MOVEMENTS

Almost half your weight is made up of muscles. They are everywhere – even in your skin, eyes and heart. Every movement you make, from blinking to leaping through the air, depends on muscles. So do the movements inside your body, such as the beating of your heart and the pushing of food through your intestines. Without muscles your body would be completely still.

When you tense a muscle it gets shorter and thicker. As it shortens it pulls whatever it is attached to. For instance, the large muscle in the back of your thigh is fixed at the top to your hip bone and at the bottom to your shin bone, just below your knee. When you shorten this muscle, it pulls your shin and so your knee bends.

Muscles can only pull. They cannot push. When you relax the muscle at the back of your thigh it becomes floppy, but it does not push your leg straight again. To do this you have to tense the muscle at the front of your thigh. This pulls the front of your shin and straightens your leg. Many muscles in your body work like this, in pairs. One pulls a part one way, and the other pulls it back again.

How far can you jump?

When you jump through the air you use far more than just your leg muscles. Your arms swing back, then up and out to help you balance. Your back straightens, then your head and body bend as you land. All these movements depend on teams of muscles shortening and then relaxing at exactly the right moment.

Taking to the air
As you take off, four sets of muscles are shortening. They straighten your hips, knees, ankles, and even your feet and toes. Muscles that work your toes are in the front of your lower leg, connected to your toes by tendons (*see pages 60-61*).

Power for the push-off
First you crouch down. Then you tense the large, powerful muscles at the front of your thighs and the back of your calves. This straightens your knees and stretches your feet for the jump.

Inside a muscle

Cut a muscle in half and you will see it is made of thick bundles. Each bundle is made of small, stringy muscle fibres. In turn, each fibre is made of even smaller fibres called fibrils.

There are also tiny nerves in a muscle, which control how much it shortens. And there are plenty of blood vessels, to supply the muscle with all the energy it needs when it is working.

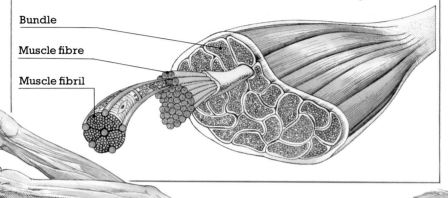

Bundle

Muscle fibre

Muscle fibril

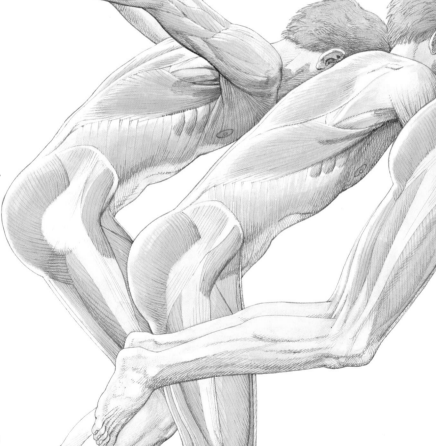

In mid-air
At the top of your jump, your leg muscles are loose and relaxed except for small adjustments to keep you balanced. As you come in to land they shorten again, ready to absorb the landing.

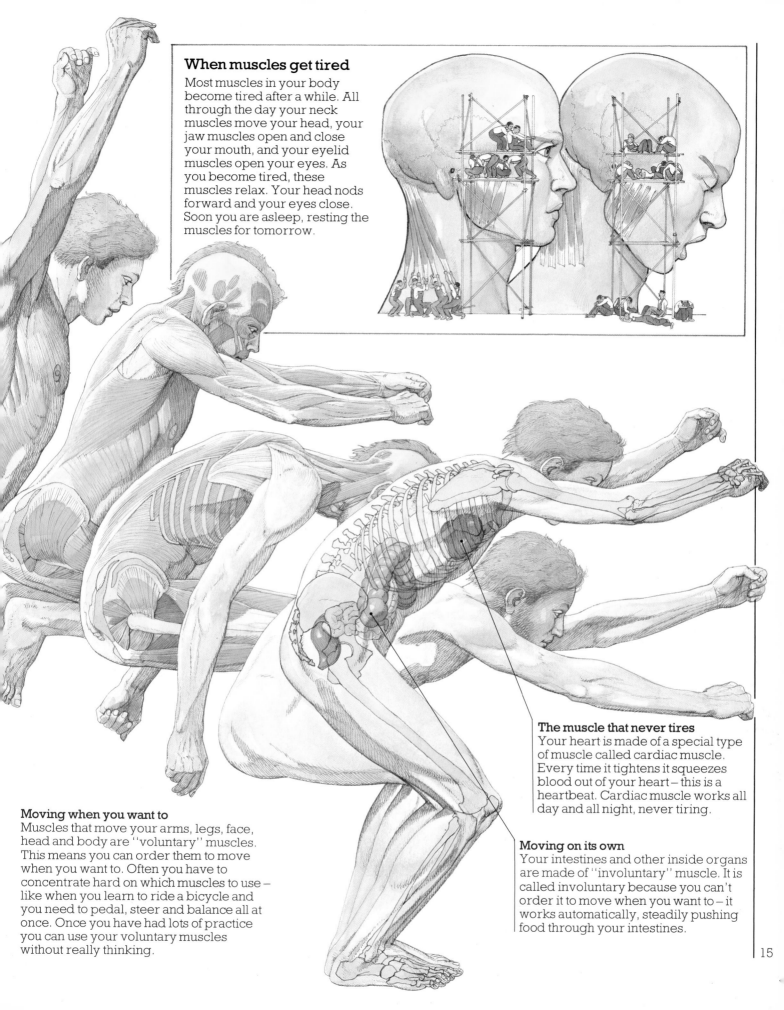

When muscles get tired

Most muscles in your body become tired after a while. All through the day your neck muscles move your head, your jaw muscles open and close your mouth, and your eyelid muscles open your eyes. As you become tired, these muscles relax. Your head nods forward and your eyes close. Soon you are asleep, resting the muscles for tomorrow.

Moving when you want to

Muscles that move your arms, legs, face, head and body are "voluntary" muscles. This means you can order them to move when you want to. Often you have to concentrate hard on which muscles to use – like when you learn to ride a bicycle and you need to pedal, steer and balance all at once. Once you have had lots of practice you can use your voluntary muscles without really thinking.

The muscle that never tires

Your heart is made of a special type of muscle called cardiac muscle. Every time it tightens it squeezes blood out of your heart – this is a heartbeat. Cardiac muscle works all day and all night, never tiring.

Moving on its own

Your intestines and other inside organs are made of "involuntary" muscle. It is called involuntary because you can't order it to move when you want to – it works automatically, steadily pushing food through your intestines.

15

BLOOD: THE BODY'S TRANSPORT SYSTEM

Your five litres (eight pints) of blood contains so many substances and does so many jobs that it is difficult to finish the list. The most important thing it does is supply oxygen and digested food to every part of your body. Also, it takes away waste chemicals to be dealt with by your lungs, liver and kidneys.

Blood carries many special chemicals around the body. It distributes the hormones that control such things as growth and sexual development. Its clotting chemicals seal cuts in your skin. Its white cells help to fight infection.

And it helps to control your body temperature (*see page 11*).

Blood flows out of the heart into tubes called arteries. These divide into branches again and again until they are too small to see. These microscopic tubes, only a hundredth of a millimetre across, are called *capillaries,* and they reach every part of your body. Their walls are so thin that oxygen and other substances can seep through them from the blood into the body tissues. The capillaries join together, become larger and form veins that take the blood back to your heart.

Watertight vessels
Your main blood vessels, the arteries and veins are watertight – or rather they are "bloodtight". Blood cannot escape from them. Only when they have divided many times to form capillaries can substances seep out of the blood, into the tissues of your body.

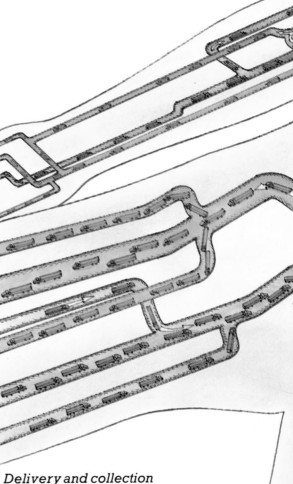

What is blood made of?
Over half of your blood is made up of a watery liquid called *plasma*, which contains dissolved chemicals like salts and food. The rest is cells. Most of them are doughnut-shaped red cells, which carry oxygen. These are small, even for cells – each one is only seven thousandths of a millimetre across. There are also white cells, which fight infection, and platelets, which help blood to clot. In a pinhead-sized drop of blood there are five million red cells, 10,000 white cells and 250,000 platelets.

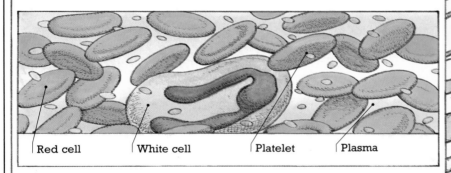

Red cell   White cell   Platelet   Plasma

How blood clots
Normally, blood cells cannot escape from their vessels (**1**). If you cut yourself, blood begins to leak out of the broken vessel (**2**). This must be stopped, or your blood could ooze away! Clotting is started by the tiny platelets floating amongst the blood cells. Quickly they begin to stick together (**3**). They form a sticky lump that traps red cells (**4**). Chemicals from the platelets react with chemicals in the blood to make a microscopic net that traps more cells. Gradually a blood clot forms (**5**), hardens and seals the cut (**6**).

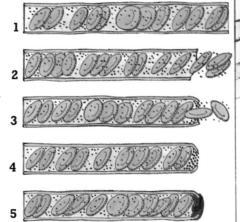

Delivery and collection
Your blood is like a transport system and runs a delivery and collection service. Every part of your body needs oxygen (the red loads in the picture), and blood takes it there, along the arteries. Every part of your body makes carbon dioxide and wastes (the blue loads). Blood carries this away along the veins, back to the heart and lungs.

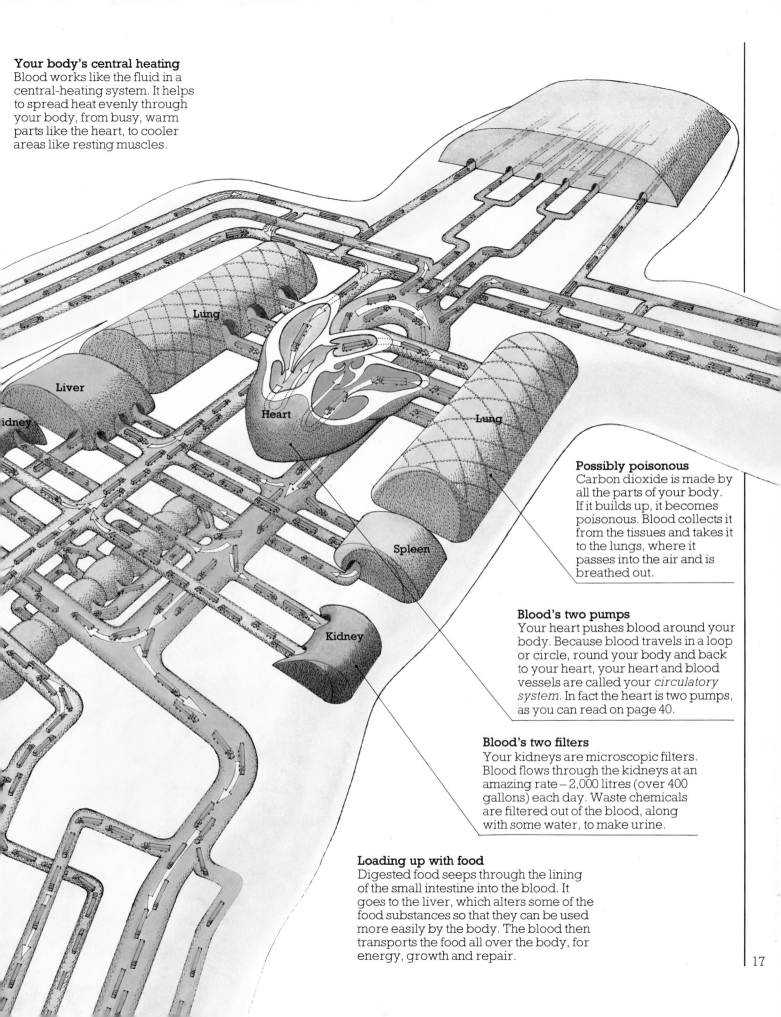

Your body's central heating
Blood works like the fluid in a central-heating system. It helps to spread heat evenly through your body, from busy, warm parts like the heart, to cooler areas like resting muscles.

Lung

Liver

idney

Heart

Lung

Spleen

Kidney

Possibly poisonous
Carbon dioxide is made by all the parts of your body. If it builds up, it becomes poisonous. Blood collects it from the tissues and takes it to the lungs, where it passes into the air and is breathed out.

Blood's two pumps
Your heart pushes blood around your body. Because blood travels in a loop or circle, round your body and back to your heart, your heart and blood vessels are called your *circulatory system*. In fact the heart is two pumps, as you can read on page 40.

Blood's two filters
Your kidneys are microscopic filters. Blood flows through the kidneys at an amazing rate – 2,000 litres (over 400 gallons) each day. Waste chemicals are filtered out of the blood, along with some water, to make urine.

Loading up with food
Digested food seeps through the lining of the small intestine into the blood. It goes to the liver, which alters some of the food substances so that they can be used more easily by the body. The blood then transports the food all over the body, for energy, growth and repair.

YOUR BONES

The bones of your skeleton give your body stiffness and support. You have about 208 bones in your body and without them you would collapse like a heap of jelly. Each bone is a certain shape and size – which is very important for the job it must do. For example, your backbone (spine) is made of 26 separate bones. Each one can bend and twist only a little by means of special joints above and below it. But over the whole backbone these small movements add up, so that you can bend over almost double and twist right round to look behind you.

Your arm and leg bones are long and strong, like girders in a building. Where they touch other bones at their ends, they are large and rounded so that they move smoothly against each other.

Some bones, such as your shoulder blades and hip bones, are large and flat, shaped like plates. They give a big area, to anchor the powerful muscles that move your arms and legs. Your breast bone is also wide and flat, to anchor the muscles that raise your chest when you breathe.

The many small bones in your hands and feet are worked by lots of muscles. This lets you make small, delicate movements such as picking up a pin or balancing on one foot. Over half your bones are in your wrists, hands, ankles and feet.

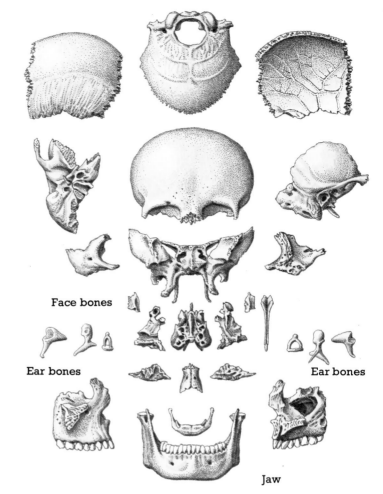

Face bones

Ear bones   **Ear bones**

Jaw

How many bones?

Count all the bones on these two pages. The human body is supposed to have about 208 bones – but where are they all?

The answer is that, as you grow, separate bones knit and fuse together solidly to form fewer, larger bones.

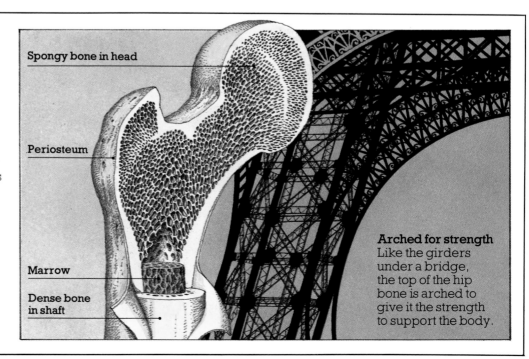

Inside a bone

Your bones are not hard, white and brittle, like the dried-out bones in museums. Bones, like the thigh bone shown here, are one-third water and are busy living tissues. They need lots of blood to supply them with food. The end or "head" of the bone is spongy inside, so as to be strong but light. The middle or "shaft" is not solid bone for the same reason. On the outside is a living "skin" called the periosteum, which forms an anchorage for the various muscles and joints that attach to the bone. On the inside of some bones is the jelly-like marrow that makes blood cells (*see pages 16-17*).

Spongy bone in head

Periosteum

Marrow

Dense bone in shaft

Arched for strength
Like the girders under a bridge, the top of the hip bone is arched to give it the strength to support the body.

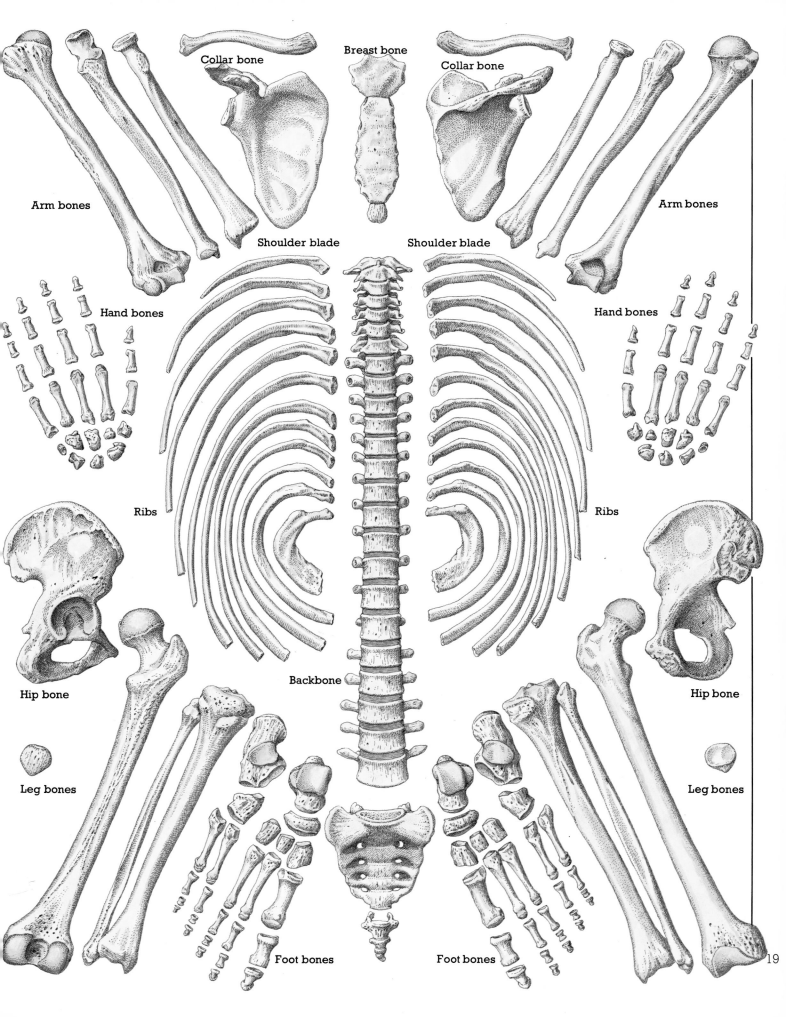

Collar bone

Breast bone

Collar bone

Arm bones

Arm bones

Shoulder blade

Shoulder blade

Hand bones

Hand bones

Ribs

Ribs

Hip bone

Hip bone

Backbone

Leg bones

Leg bones

Foot bones

Foot bones

19

THE BODY'S FRAMEWORK

Any large structure, like a building or crane or bridge, needs a framework to support it. This is usually made of girders. The architects and engineers design each girder to do a certain job. Where there is a lot of strain, thick strong girders are needed. Where stresses are small, thin girders are best because they weigh less. The bones of your body are like girders, but in many ways they are better. Bone is a living material and can change according to your body's needs. If extra stresses and strains are put on a bone, it can grow and thicken and become stronger. This sometimes happens to the bones of athletes, horse-riders and weightlifters. If a bone breaks in an accident, the broken parts slowly join together again and the bone mends itself. (It is best if a doctor puts the broken parts back into the right positions, so that they knit together in the same shape as the original bone.) Bone also acts as a mineral store. If minerals in food are in short supply, bones release some of their minerals for more important uses elsewhere in the body.

The skeleton skyscraper
Imagine making a huge human body. If you build a skyscraper or an office block you begin with a framework of girders. In the same way, a body needs a framework – the skeleton. This has two main jobs. It has to be a strong support for the softer parts which will be added later and it also has to protect some of these softer parts from damage.

Protecting your nerves
In many bones there are small holes and grooves for nerves and blood vessels. The long bones in your arm have shallow grooves in them. Nerves lie in these grooves. If the nerves lay on top of the bones, they could be damaged, as the muscles in your arm would press them against the bone when they tightened.

Waving and running
The long bones in your arms and legs are thin in the middle, where there is the least stress and strain. This helps keep them as light as possible, so you can move them more easily.

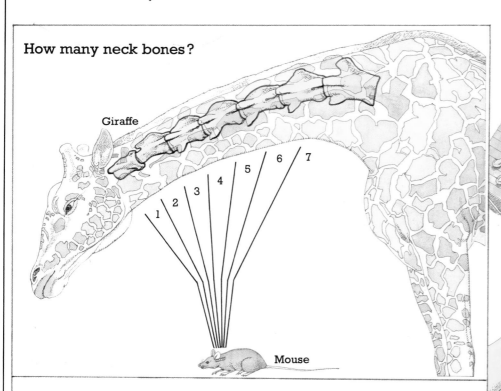

How many neck bones?

Giraffe

1 2 3 4 5 6 7

Mouse

All furry animals have roughly the same number of bones in their skeleton, but these bones are different shapes and sizes.

The animal with the longest neck, the giraffe, has seven neck bones – the same number as a tiny animal like a mouse (and the same as you).

Eleven bones make three
Each of your two large hip bones is made from three separate bones fused together. Together with the five bones fused in your sacrum (*see page 44*), they make a "ring" of eleven bones.

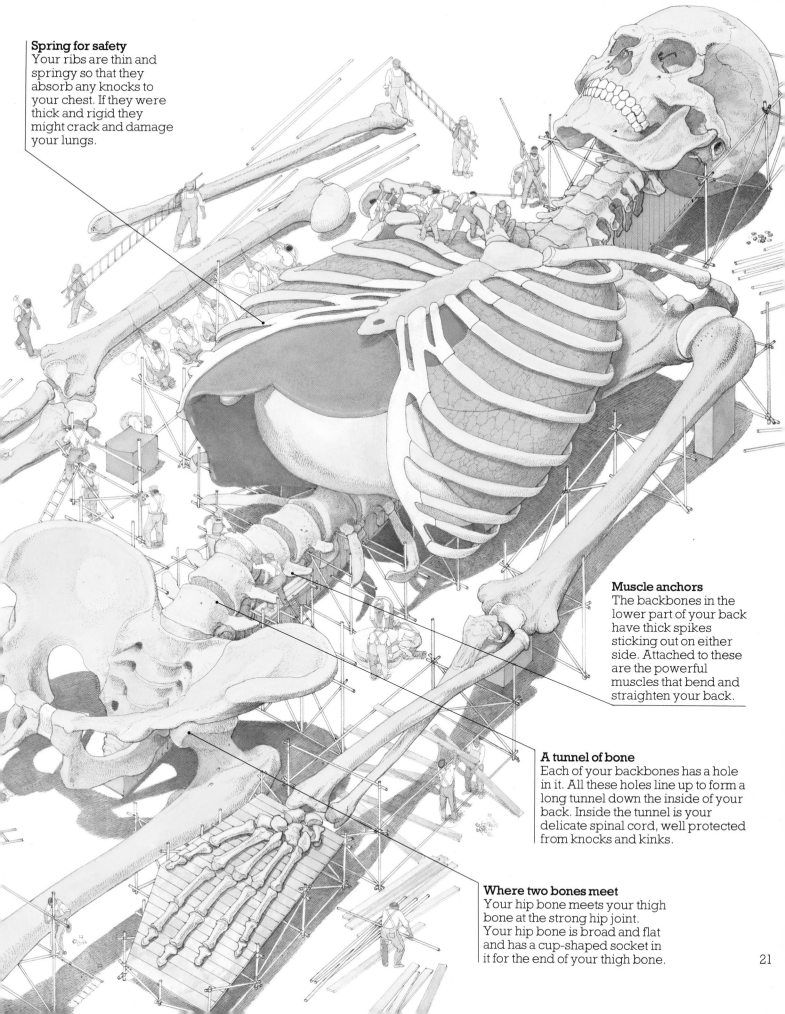

Spring for safety
Your ribs are thin and springy so that they absorb any knocks to your chest. If they were thick and rigid they might crack and damage your lungs.

Muscle anchors
The backbones in the lower part of your back have thick spikes sticking out on either side. Attached to these are the powerful muscles that bend and straighten your back.

A tunnel of bone
Each of your backbones has a hole in it. All these holes line up to form a long tunnel down the inside of your back. Inside the tunnel is your delicate spinal cord, well protected from knocks and kinks.

Where two bones meet
Your hip bone meets your thigh bone at the strong hip joint. Your hip bone is broad and flat and has a cup-shaped socket in it for the end of your thigh bone.

21

THE HEAD

Thinking, seeing, hearing, smelling, tasting, eating, drinking – and taking in air. The various parts that do these vital jobs are all packed into your head. There are good reasons why the main sense organs (eyes, nose and tongue) are near your mouth, where you take in food. Your eyes can look closely at what you eat, your nose can check

A hollow for the eye
This deep, rounded hole in your skull bone protects your eye from injury yet still lets it swivel in any direction.

A box for the brain
The upper part of your skull is the cranium or "brain box", a strong case made of eight curved bones fixed together.

The far-seeing eye
Up near the top of your body, your eyes are on a "watch-tower" that gives you a good view of your surroundings.

The all-knowing brain
The brain, the control centre of your body, receives information from your eyes, ears, nose and mouth.

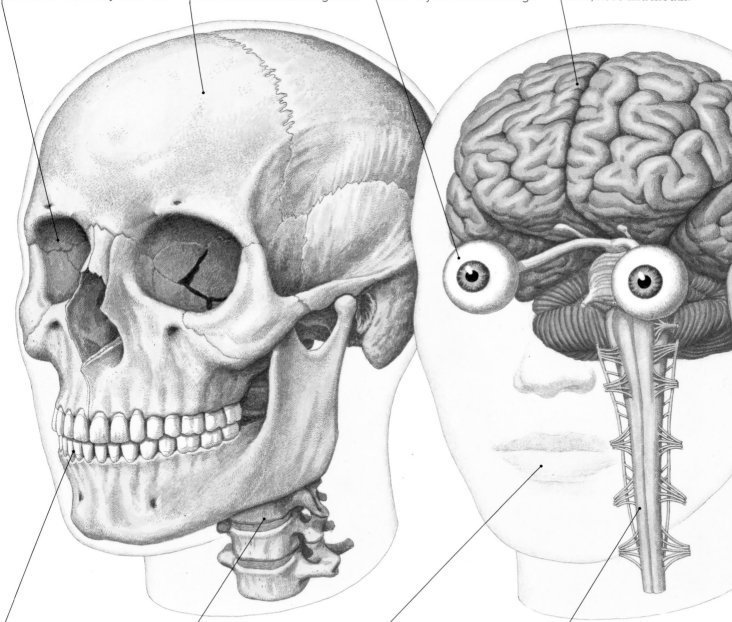

Chopping and chewing
Digestion starts here. Your teeth are firmly anchored in sockets in the skull and jaw bones. They cut off pieces of food and chew them into soft, easily swallowed lumps.

Saying yes – or no
Your top two backbones (vertebrae) are special. The upper one lets you nod your head up and down. The lower one lets you shake your head from side to side.

Facial control
Your face is full of nerves that connect to your brain and spinal cord. They control every movement, from eating a meal to licking your lips afterwards.

Linking brain and body
Your spinal cord is like an extension of your brain into your body. In a grown-up it is about 45 cms (18 ins) long yet weighs only 30 gms (just over 1 oz).

its smell, while the taste buds on your tongue detect its flavour. This all helps to make sure that you don't eat bad food and make yourself ill. Also your nose can smell the air you breathe, to make sure it is not stale or bad. There is also a good reason why your head is perched on top of your body. It's in the best position to look around, listen for sounds and sniff for smells. Your neck is flexible so that you can look up and down and turn your head easily. If your head was near your feet you would not be able to see very far, and you'd always be breathing in dust!

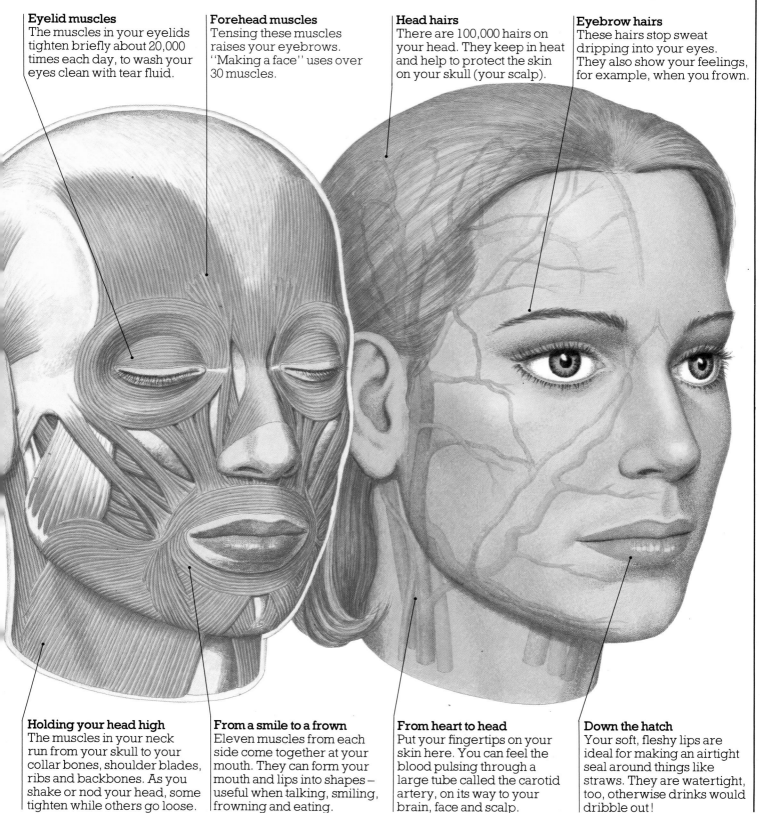

Eyelid muscles
The muscles in your eyelids tighten briefly about 20,000 times each day, to wash your eyes clean with tear fluid.

Forehead muscles
Tensing these muscles raises your eyebrows. "Making a face" uses over 30 muscles.

Head hairs
There are 100,000 hairs on your head. They keep in heat and help to protect the skin on your skull (your scalp).

Eyebrow hairs
These hairs stop sweat dripping into your eyes. They also show your feelings, for example, when you frown.

Holding your head high
The muscles in your neck run from your skull to your collar bones, shoulder blades, ribs and backbones. As you shake or nod your head, some tighten while others go loose.

From a smile to a frown
Eleven muscles from each side come together at your mouth. They can form your mouth and lips into shapes — useful when talking, smiling, frowning and eating.

From heart to head
Put your fingertips on your skin here. You can feel the blood pulsing through a large tube called the carotid artery, on its way to your brain, face and scalp.

Down the hatch
Your soft, fleshy lips are ideal for making an airtight seal around things like straws. They are watertight, too, otherwise drinks would dribble out!

23

THE BRAIN

Many years ago, people thought that the heart controlled the body. They believed that feelings and emotions were based in the heart, since when you are frightened or worried you can feel your heart thumping. This is why we have sayings like "I know in my heart that it is true". But they were wrong. Today, we know that the heart is just a muscular pump for the blood. The heart is controlled by the brain. In fact, the whole body is controlled by the brain.

The brain is a pinky-grey, blancmange-like organ weighing around one and a half kilograms (three pounds). It has grooves and folds on the outside, and inside it is hollow and filled with fluid. It does not look very remarkable. Even under a powerful microscope all you can see is a tangle of nerve cells. Only recently have scientists begun to discover how the brain's nerve cells are connected to each other and how they work together.

The brain makes up about one-fiftieth of the body's weight. Yet it uses up one-fifth of the body's energy. This amazing organ is more complicated than any computer you can think of. And that's what your brain does – think. Your brain holds your memories, feelings and emotions. It is where you learn and know, guess and have ideas – in short, it holds your mind.

Inside the brain

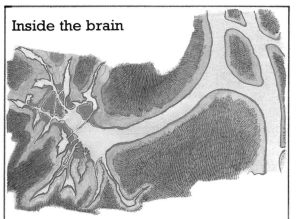

Your brain is made almost entirely of nerve cells (*see page 12*), perhaps 10,000 million of them. Each one has many thin "fingers" (*dendrites*) along which it can send signals to other nerve cells. Which route a signal takes along the dendrites depends on what it means. Each nerve cell connects with thousands of others, so the possible number of routes a signal could take around the network is mind-boggling.

Inside your body's headquarters
Different parts of your brain do different jobs, like the various offices at the headquarters of a large company. But the differences are not as clear-cut as in an office block. Memories, for example, do not seem to be stored in any one part of the brain, but all over it.

Your memory banks
No one really knows how the brain remembers. Each memory might be stored as a chemical substance or as a special nerve circuit between certain nerve cells. Some memories only last for a few minutes; others can last all of your life.

Your sorting office
Your thalamus, deep inside your brain, acts as a kind of sorting office. It receives the messages coming in from your body and senses, then sends them on to whichever part of your brain they need to go to.

Running on automatic
Your body has an "automatic pilot". It is your brain stem, the lower part of your brain near your spinal cord. It runs many parts of your body automatically. Your heart beats and your lungs breathe without your having to think about them at all.

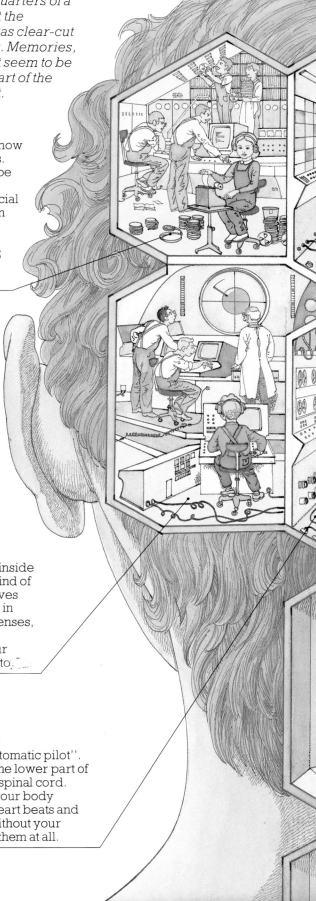

Central control
The largest part of your brain is the cortex (*shown on the next page*). This is where incoming messages are sifted and decisions taken about what to do. If action is needed, messages are sent out from the cortex to the part of your body concerned.

Messages in
Every minute your brain receives millions of nerve signals from your body. Important information must be quickly sorted out from run-of-the-mill messages. The distant sound of traffic might not be very interesting – but the smell of burning could be vital.

Brain and body
Your spinal cord links your brain to your body. Your brain and spinal cord together make up your *central nervous system*. Nerves branch out from the base of your brain and from your spinal cord and go to every part of your body, carrying signals and messages to and fro. These nerves make up your *peripheral nervous system*.

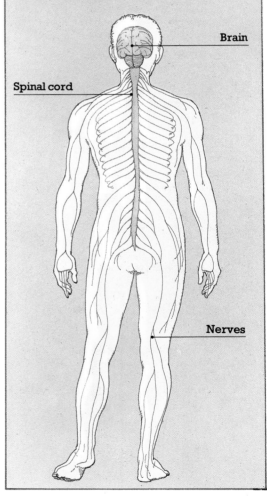

Brain

Spinal cord

Nerves

Messages out
Millions of nerve signals leave the brain every minute, going to your muscles and telling them what to do. Learning a new activity, such as riding a bicycle, needs great concentration. With practice you can do it without really thinking. The same thing happened when you learned to walk and talk.

THE BRAIN MAP

The main parts of your brain are the two *cerebral cortexes*. Scientists have discovered that certain parts of the cortex deal with signals coming in from certain parts of the body. Other parts control signals going out. We can draw a "map" on the cortex showing which part, or centre, of the brain is linked to which part of the body. However, the centres are not in the same positions as the parts of your body. The map is all jumbled up.

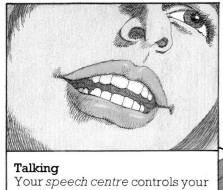

Talking
Your *speech centre* controls your voice box and mouth muscles.

Thinking
Thoughts and feelings are spread over the front of your cortex.

Your body on your brain
This drawing of the brain "map" is from the left side. The eye is in its real position on the left, with the brain stem (which connects to the spinal cord) at the bottom of the picture.

Hearing
Messages from your ears are dealt with in your *hearing centre*.

The two sides of the brain

Did you know that the left side of your brain is linked to the right side of your body? Nerves connecting to your brain and spinal cord cross to the opposite side, so when you move your right arm, the signals telling you to move it are coming from the left side of your brain. Also, the two halves of the brain do not work in exactly the same way. In most people the left side of the brain is better at dealing with words and numbers and sorting out problems. The right side is better at artistic and musical activities and generally being creative.

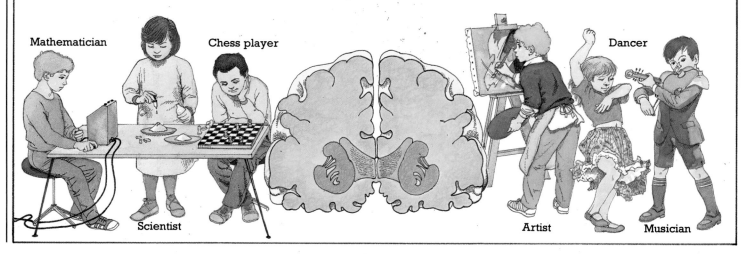

Mathematician　　Chess player　　　　　　　　　　Dancer

Scientist　　　　　　　　　　　　　　　　　　Artist　　Musician

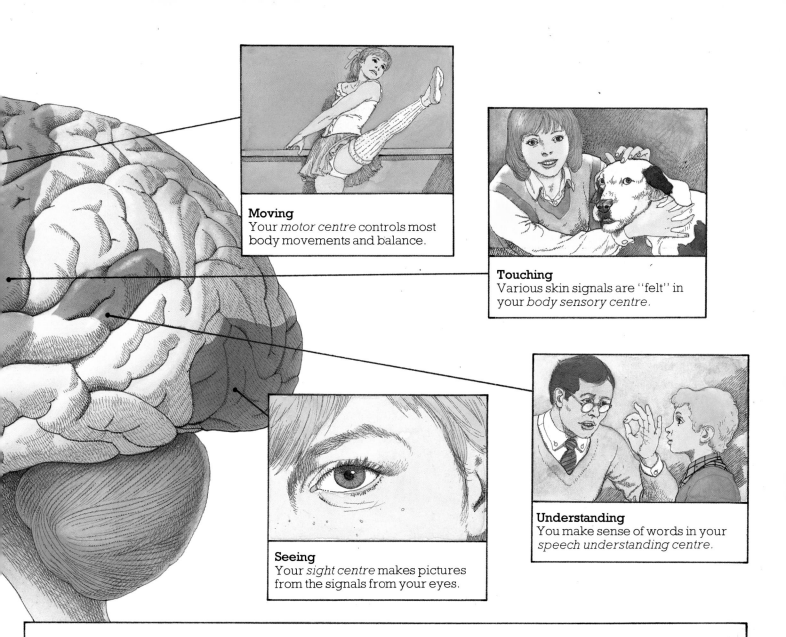

Moving
Your *motor centre* controls most body movements and balance.

Touching
Various skin signals are "felt" in your *body sensory centre.*

Understanding
You make sense of words in your *speech understanding centre.*

Seeing
Your *sight centre* makes pictures from the signals from your eyes.

Animal brains

Different animals have brains of various shapes and sizes. By studying which parts of the brain are best developed in a certain animal, and how that animal lives, we can gain an idea of what that part does.

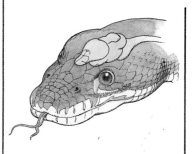

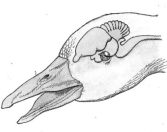

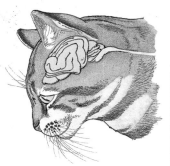

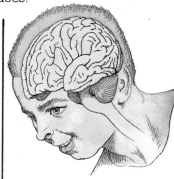

Snake
The snake's brain has three main parts, each about the same size. The back part controls basic processes such as heartbeat.

Bird
A bird does not think, but the middle part of its brain is highly developed. This part controls the bird's wide range of movements.

Mammal
In a cat the front parts of the brain are much bigger. These are involved in thinking behaviour – what we call "intelligence".

Human
In our brains the front parts (*cerebral hemispheres*) are so big that they cover almost all other parts. This explains our great intelligence.

27

TOUCH AND SENSES

How do you find out about the world around you? You look, listen, smell, taste and touch. These are called your five senses, and your eyes, ears, nose, tongue and skin are your main sense organs. Over the next eight pages you can see how these senses work and how important they are to you.

In fact you have more than five senses. The sense of touch is really several different senses. You can feel light touch, heavy pressure, heat and cold, movements and vibrations and pain.

There is a different sense of "feeling", inside your muscles, which tells you how relaxed or contracted they are. Using this sense (the "position sense") you can tell what positions your body, arms and legs are in without looking. You can close your eyes and touch each fingertip in turn.

Another of your senses helps you to stand upright and not fall down – your sense of balance. Balance is a combination of what the balance organs in your ears tell you (*see page 33*), plus what your eyes see, plus what your skin and muscles feel (especially the soles of your feet).

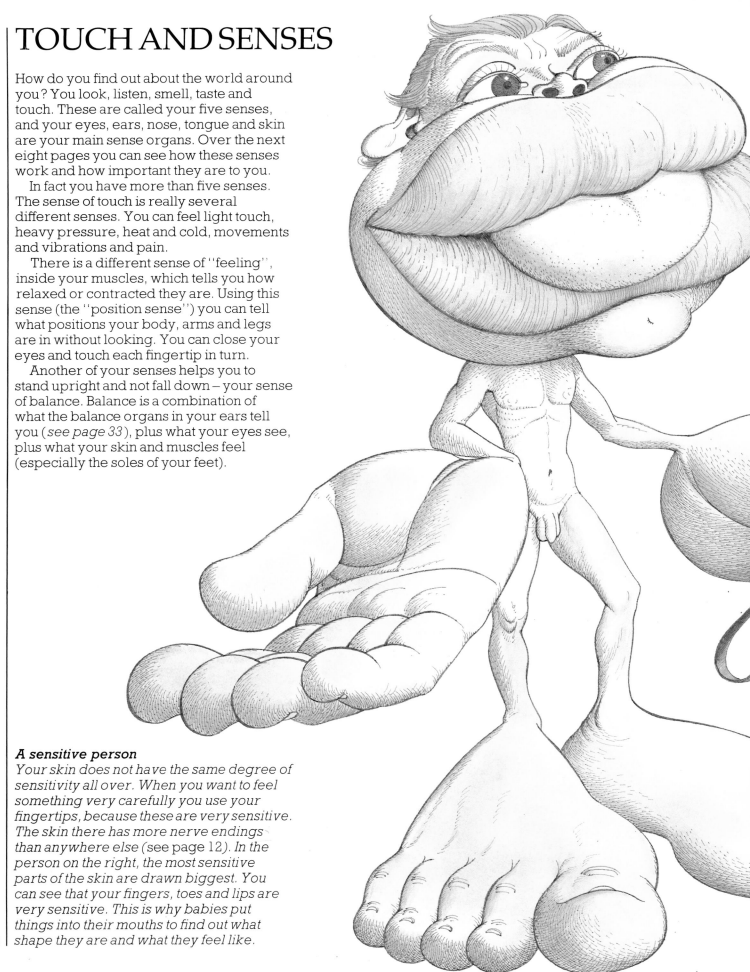

A sensitive person
Your skin does not have the same degree of sensitivity all over. When you want to feel something very carefully you use your fingertips, because these are very sensitive. The skin there has more nerve endings than anywhere else (see page 12). In the person on the right, the most sensitive parts of the skin are drawn biggest. You can see that your fingers, toes and lips are very sensitive. This is why babies put things into their mouths to find out what shape they are and what they feel like.

Keeping in touch

Your skin tells you about much more than just the shape and texture of the things you touch. There are many different kinds of nerve endings just under the surface of your skin, which tell you different things about the outside world.

You can feel heat or cold. For instance, you can tell whether the air around you is warm or cool. When water splashes on you, you feel a combination of touch and cold. Sometimes you feel only light touch, as when you walk on a sandy beach and the grains of sand press evenly all over the soles of your feet. But when you come to sharp pebbles, the edges of the pebbles press hard on your feet. This can be very uncomfortable. If any pressure becomes too heavy it begins to hurt, because it sets off special nerve endings deep in your skin. This is your sense of pain telling you that your body is in danger of being damaged.

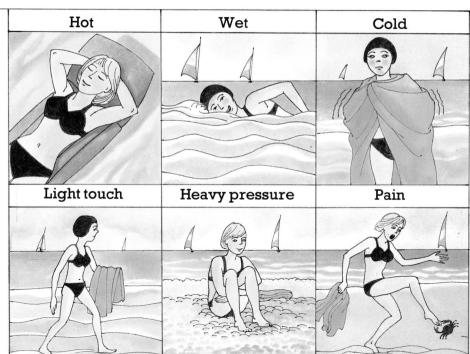

Hot — Wet — Cold — Light touch — Heavy pressure — Pain

How animals sense the world

Different animals sense their surroundings in different ways. Each part of this dog and cat is drawn according to how sensitive it is. The dog's large nose shows it has a very good sense of smell, and its whiskers can feel well. Its big tongue means it has a keen sense of taste. A dog's eyes are not that good, especially compared to the cat, whose enormous eyes show that it has very sharp sight. The cat's huge ears mean it can hear well too. All this is for a reason. Cats hunt at night, so they need good eyes and ears in the dark. Dogs hunt mainly by sniffing around for scent.

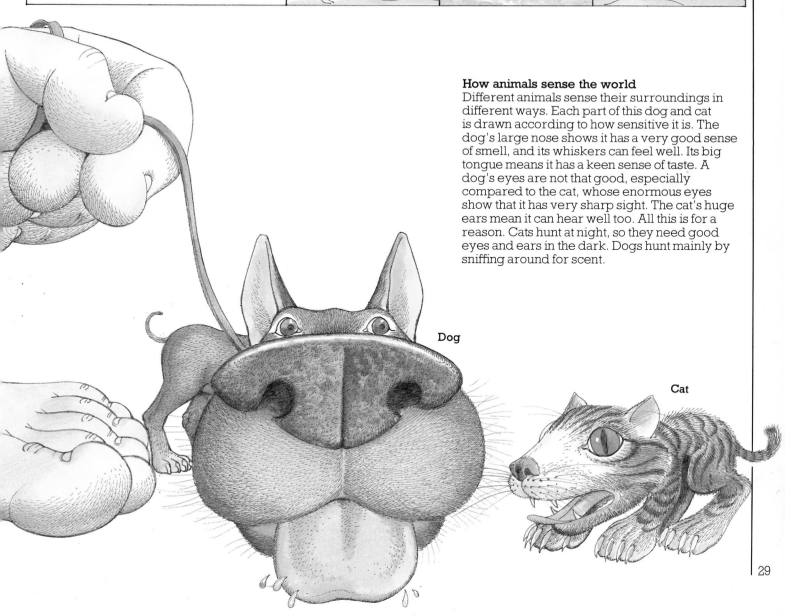

Dog

Cat

THE EYE

Of all our senses, our eyes are the most important. A scientist worked out that four-fifths of everything you remember was something you had seen, from the beauty of the sun setting behind mountains, to learning sums at school.

Even more amazing is that your picture of the world is only slightly larger than a postage stamp. This is the area inside your eye where the picture is detected by nerve cells. These nerve cells are spread out in the *retina*, which lines the inside of the eye. There are two special types of cell, called *rods* and *cones*.

There are over 100 million rods in each eye. They see in black and white (not colour) and work well in poor light. There are about seven million cones in each eye. The cones see colours and fine details, but only work in bright light. Each time light hits a rod or cone it generates a nerve signal, which travels out of your eye and along the main nerve to your brain. At the brain's sight centre (*see page 27*) all these impulses are sorted out and put together. The black-and-white and colour pictures are combined, as are the pictures from your two eyes. The eye simply turns light rays into nerve impulses and sends them on. It is in your brain that you actually "see".

Seeing in cinema-scope
Like a giant cinema screen, the front part of your eye projects a picture of what is outside on to the back part. The pictures move all the time. Even when you try to stare steadily, your eyes still dart about.

A clear view
The curved part at the front of the eye is the *cornea*. It is crystal clear, and its shape bends light rays as they pass through, helping the lens to focus them. The very thin layer on the surface of the cornea is the *conjunctiva*. This is also clear and it is very sensitive, feeling when the smallest bit of dust lands on it.

A sharp picture
Like a camera, the eye has to focus so that the picture you see is clear and sharp. The *lens* at the front of the eye does the focusing. Muscles around it tighten and pull it thinner or relax to let it get fatter. A thin lens focuses faraway objects, while a fat lens focuses near ones.

Just enough light
The coloured part of your eye is called the *iris*. It controls the amount of light entering your eye, by making the hole in its centre larger or smaller. In dim light the hole is large. In bright light it goes very small, to protect the sensitive nerve cells at the back of your eye.

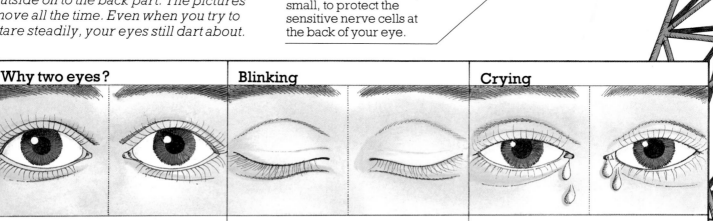

Why two eyes?	Blinking	Crying
Each eye sees a slightly different view of an object – close one eye then the other, to see the difference. Also the eyes swivel in to look at nearby things but look straight ahead at distant things. The brain uses this information to judge distance.	For about half an hour each day you cannot see – you are blinking. Your eyelids sweep across the delicate eye surface and spread a fresh film of tear fluid. This washes dust and germs from the eye. A blink lasts for about one-third of a second.	No one knows why we cry. Your eyes "water" when they get bits in them, to wash them clean. Tear fluid normally goes down the tiny holes in the inner parts of the eyelid, into the nose. This is why you blow your nose when you have been crying.

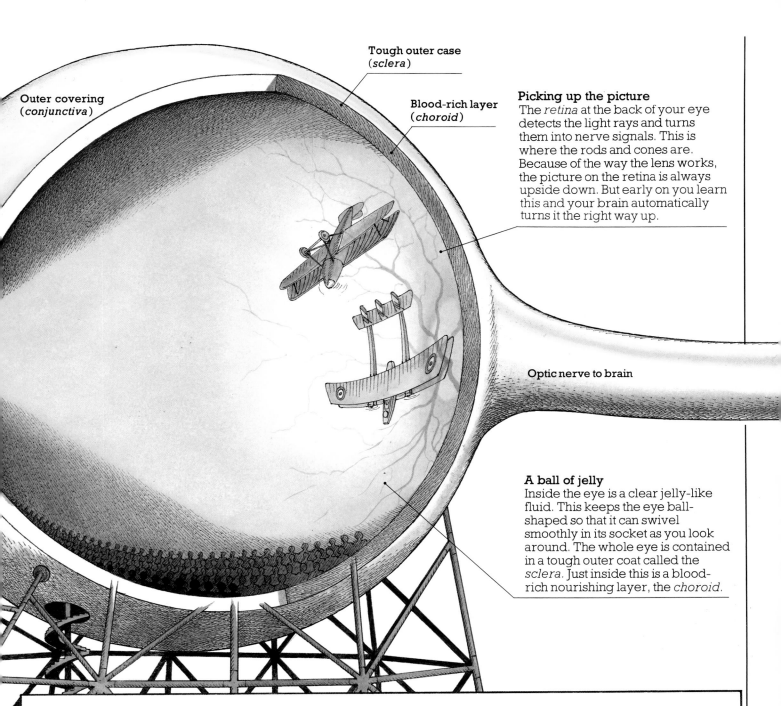

Outer covering
(*conjunctiva*)

Tough outer case
(*sclera*)

Blood-rich layer
(*choroid*)

Picking up the picture
The *retina* at the back of your eye detects the light rays and turns them into nerve signals. This is where the rods and cones are. Because of the way the lens works, the picture on the retina is always upside down. But early on you learn this and your brain automatically turns it the right way up.

Optic nerve to brain

A ball of jelly
Inside the eye is a clear jelly-like fluid. This keeps the eye ball-shaped so that it can swivel smoothly in its socket as you look around. The whole eye is contained in a tough outer coat called the *sclera*. Just inside this is a blood-rich nourishing layer, the *choroid*.

Animal eyes

Different animals see the world in various ways. Humans have quite good vision compared to many other animals. Maybe our ancestors hunted and found ripe fruits and other foods mainly by sight, rather than by smell.

Seeing in the dark
An owl hunts at night. Its eyes are enormous, to collect what little light there is. They also face forwards, to judge distance accurately.

Keeping all-round watch
A mouse is active mainly at dawn and dusk, so its eyes are large too. They stick out from its head so that it can keep watch for danger all around.

Hundreds of eyes
An insect has two "eyes", each made of hundreds of tiny flat parts. It probably sees the world like a mosaic, in tiny overlapping segments.

THE EAR

Imagine dozing in a field in the summer sun. Suddenly a jet plane roars overhead. As the noise fades away, you can hear the quiet humming of bees and the birds singing in the distance. The jet makes a noise a million million million times louder than the bees and birds – but your ears can hear them both. You can also hear sounds ranging from the low notes of a double bass to the high sound of a cymbal.

The part of the ear you can see is called the outer ear. This simply collects sound waves and funnels them into your ear canal. The important parts of your ear are buried 3 or 4 centimetres (1½ inches) inside your head, just behind and below your eye. These inner parts are well protected, surrounded by your skull bone. They turn sound waves into electrical nerve signals and send them to your brain. In your brain the signals are sorted out and you "hear".

Having two ears is very useful. If a sound comes from one side, the sound waves reach one ear a split second before they get to the other. Your brain detects this time difference and can tell you where the sound is coming from.

Music to your ears
Your ear is an amazing and delicate organ. It can hear all the complicated sound waves made by an orchestra. It can detect loudness (volume) and high and low notes (pitch). From the signals it sends to your brain, you can pick out the sound of each instrument even when they are all being played at the same time.

Your ear trumpet
Your outer ear is made of the ear flap on the outside and your ear canal, a tube leading inwards. Many animals move their ears to detect where a sound comes from. People can't, although some can wiggle their ears.

A sticky problem
The skin on the inside of your ear canal makes a sticky substance called ear wax. Floating dust and dirt stick to it, keeping your inner ear clean. As you chew and talk, your face muscles move the lining of the canal and gradually any old wax works its way out.

Banging the drum
When you bang a drum, it shakes or *vibrates* and makes the air around it move, forming sound waves. Your eardrum works in the opposite way. Sound waves hit it and make it vibrate. The vibrations pass along three tiny bones, the hammer, anvil and stirrup (notice their shapes).

The ear machine
Sounds go through many different forms before they reach your brain. They start out as sound waves in the air, then change to vibrating solids – your eardrum and the three tiny bones. Then they pass into the fluid inside your inner ear, in the cochlea. Finally they are converted to electrical signals and sent along nerves to your brain. A home-made model of the ear might look something like this:

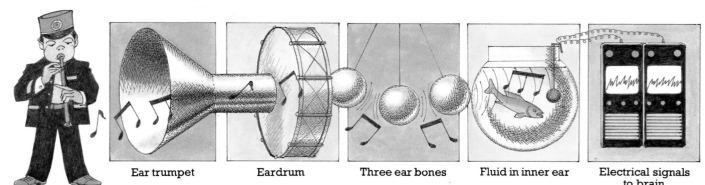

| Ear trumpet | Eardrum | Three ear bones | Fluid in inner ear | Electrical signals to brain |

Semi-circular canals

The curly tube that hears
The inner part of your ear is extremely complicated. The large snail-shaped tube is called the *cochlea*. It contains nerve cells which have tiny hairs sticking into a fluid. Vibrations passed on by the three tiny bones move the fluid, which moves the hairs, which makes nerve signals. There are over 20,000 nerve cells in each ear, and up to 100 hairs on each cell. Different parts of the cochlea can detect high and low notes.

Nerves to brain

Three ear bones

Keeping your balance
Your ears not only hear – they also help you to keep your balance. The semi-circular canals in the big picture contain fluid. As your head tilts, the fluid swirls about and tiny hair cells (like the ones in the cochlea) detect its movements. There are also tiny blobs of crystals on the hairs, like balls on bendy sticks. As you change position, gravity pulls the blobs down and bends the hairs, and this sends signals to your brain, telling it which way up you are.

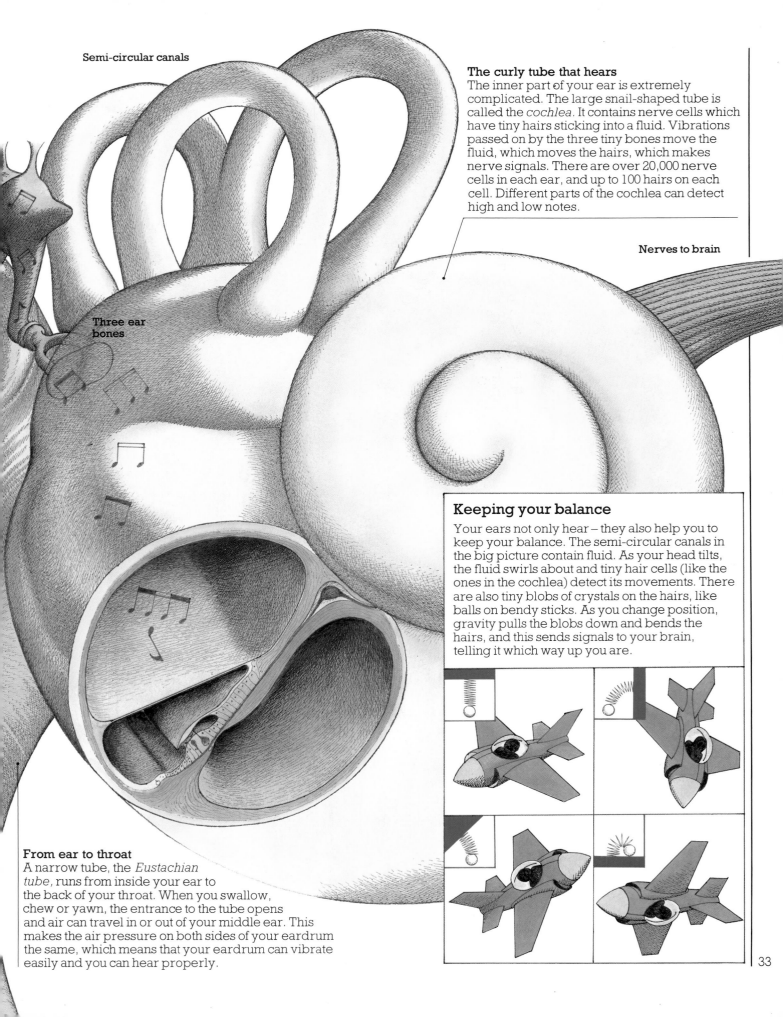

From ear to throat
A narrow tube, the *Eustachian tube,* runs from inside your ear to the back of your throat. When you swallow, chew or yawn, the entrance to the tube opens and air can travel in or out of your middle ear. This makes the air pressure on both sides of your eardrum the same, which means that your eardrum can vibrate easily and you can hear properly.

INSIDE YOUR MOUTH

Your mouth is the first stop for the food you eat. Each part of it does a certain job. Your teeth chop, chew and crush large pieces of food into small ones. Your tongue moves lumps of food around so that your teeth can get at them, and it pushes the lumps to the back of your mouth when you are ready to swallow them. Your salivary glands make a watery liquid that moistens food so that it slips easily down to your stomach. And your whole mouth warms up cold food and cools down hot food. Everything you put into your mouth is changed into small, soggy lumps that you can swallow. All this helps you to digest your food more easily later on. Your mouth has another important job. It shapes the sounds from your voice box (in your throat) into words. Try making the same noise and moving your lips, tongue, teeth and cheeks to see how many different sounds you can make.

The food processors

Inside your mouth it is dark, moist and warm. These are good conditions for germs, which feed on any old bits of food. Although the germs don't make you very ill, they can help to make your teeth bad. This is why you should clean your teeth after meals.

Grooves in the gum
Your gums help to hold your teeth securely in their sockets. There is a groove around each tooth, where the gum is joined to it. This is a favourite place for germs to lurk.

Choppers
Your four front teeth at the top and bottom are called incisors. They are sharp and chop off bits of food when you bite. Next to them are canines, which are more pointed but still good choppers.

Crushers
The rest of your teeth, towards the back of your mouth, are broad and flat. They crush and chew food. The three big teeth on each side at the very back are molars. The two in front are premolars.

Inside a tooth
Here is one of your crushing teeth, a molar, cut away to show what is inside. The top part of the tooth, above the gum, is the crown. The lower parts, the roots, anchor the tooth firmly in your jaw bone. The tooth's outer layer is enamel, the hardest substance in your body. This is just as well since it has to crunch through nuts and other tough foods. Inside is a layer of dentine, which is quite hard but can absorb bumps and knocks. Enamel and dentine have no blood vessels or nerves, so cannot feel anything. Inside the dentine is the pulp. This has many blood vessels and nerves. If you have toothache, it is because something has gone through both the enamel and the dentine and is affecting the nerves in the pulp.

Crown

Enamel

Dentine

Pulp

Gum

Blood vessels

Nerves

Root

Jaw bone

Mouthwatering
Saliva is a watery liquid made by glands under your jaws, in front of your ears and under your tongue. It helps you to digest and swallow your food. It also helps to keep your mouth and teeth clean.

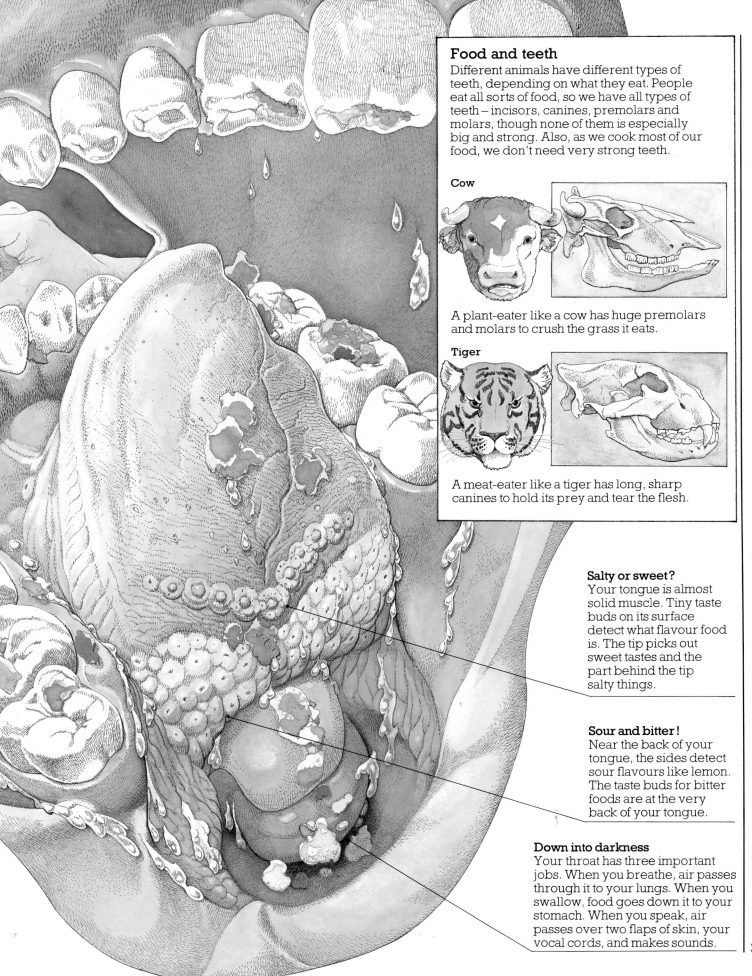

Food and teeth

Different animals have different types of teeth, depending on what they eat. People eat all sorts of food, so we have all types of teeth – incisors, canines, premolars and molars, though none of them is especially big and strong. Also, as we cook most of our food, we don't need very strong teeth.

Cow

A plant-eater like a cow has huge premolars and molars to crush the grass it eats.

Tiger

A meat-eater like a tiger has long, sharp canines to hold its prey and tear the flesh.

Salty or sweet?

Your tongue is almost solid muscle. Tiny taste buds on its surface detect what flavour food is. The tip picks out sweet tastes and the part behind the tip salty things.

Sour and bitter!

Near the back of your tongue, the sides detect sour flavours like lemon. The taste buds for bitter foods are at the very back of your tongue.

Down into darkness

Your throat has three important jobs. When you breathe, air passes through it to your lungs. When you swallow, food goes down it to your stomach. When you speak, air passes over two flaps of skin, your vocal cords, and makes sounds.

35

THE CHEST

Your chest is the powerhouse of your body. Every few seconds, every hour of every day, your chest muscles contract to make your lungs breathe in air. The oxygen in the air passes through your lungs into your blood. The blood flows to your heart. Your heart then pumps this fresh blood all around your body – every second, every

Bone and blade
Your collar bone at the front, and your shoulder blade at the back, anchor the many muscles that move your arm. You can swing your arm right round in a circle.

A rod at the back
The part of the backbone at the back of your chest is quite stiff compared to the other parts of the backbone. This helps to hold your lungs properly, for easy breathing.

Well-oiled breathing
Your lungs are covered by two thin, smooth layers of tissue with a slippery fluid like oil between them. This helps to make breathing movements easier.

A place for your heart
Your heart is slightly to the left side of your body. Your left lung is a little smaller than your right lung, as it has a slight hollow in it where your heart sits.

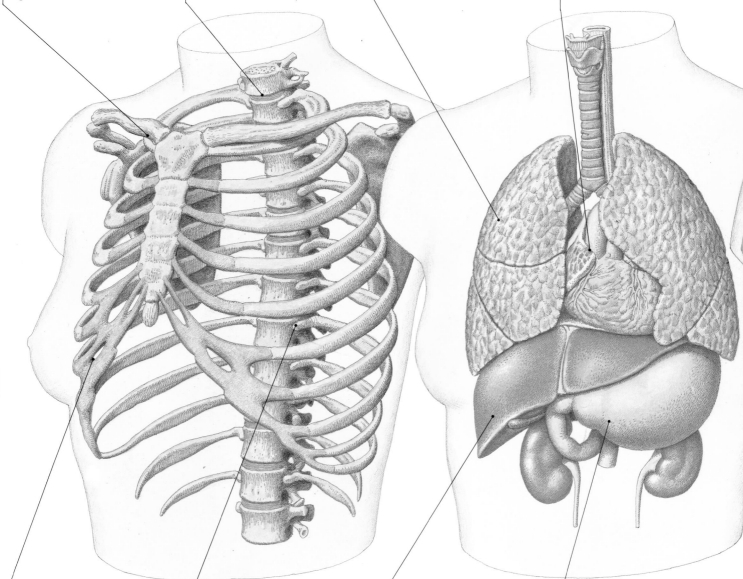

A cage at the front
Your ribs make a strong cage that protects your lungs and heart inside. But they are also hinged, so that they can move up and down as you breathe in and out.

Spare ribs
Most people have 12 pairs of ribs, but some have 11 or 13 pairs. Each pair joins to a vertebra (backbone) at the back. Only the top 7 pairs join to your breast bone.

Record-breaking liver
Your liver is your largest and busiest organ. It deals with at least 500 different body chemicals, and produces much of the heat that keeps your body warm.

Second stop for food
Your stomach carries on the job started by your mouth. It pummels your food into a pulp and churns it up with powerful chemicals, for three hours or more.

hour of every day. All the parts of your body need a never-ending supply of fresh blood, carrying plentiful oxygen. Without it, life would soon stop. Because your lungs and heart are right next to each other, blood has hardly any distance to go after it is refreshed, before it is pumped to the rest of your body. This means your body receives the freshest blood possible.

Some of your digestive organs, such as your liver and stomach, stick up inside your rib cage. They nestle under a dome-shaped sheet of muscle called your *diaphragm* which you use to breathe.

Muscles under muscles
There are several layers of muscles around your chest. They each do slightly different jobs. This one helps to pull your shoulder down and forwards.

Muscles over muscles
This large sheet-like muscle is just under your skin. It is very strong – it pulls your arm forward and can help to lift your body when you are hanging from a bar.

Making milk
In women, the breasts are large glands that make milk to feed a newborn baby. Men also have these glands but they are extremely small and do not make milk.

Blood for the brain
Deep in your chest, arteries divide and run upwards to supply blood to your arms, head and brain. Another artery arches over and goes down behind your heart.

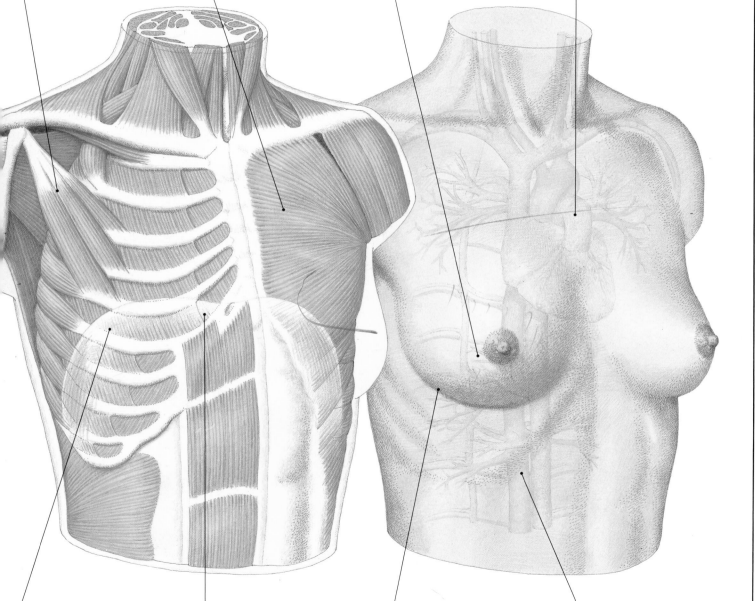

A dome that pulls down
The dome-shaped sheet of muscle under your chest is your diaphragm. When it contracts it pulls your lungs down, making them bigger, and you breathe in.

Holes in the dome
There are gaps in the diaphragm for important tubes, such as the gullet taking food to your stomach and blood vessels running to and from your heart.

Padded for protection
A layer of fat and skin cover the chest to protect it. As in other parts of the body, women usually have slightly more fatty tissue under their skin than men.

Blood for your lower half
Two large blood vessels run between your chest and abdomen. The main artery carries fresh blood down, while the main vein brings stale blood back to the heart.

THE LUNGS

How long can you hold your breath? A minute, or even two? Much longer and your body tells you to start breathing again, because breathing brings fresh air into it and this contains oxygen, which is vital for you to keep living.

Your lungs are superbly designed to absorb as much oxygen as possible from the air. They also get rid of the waste substance carbon dioxide. When you breathe in, air contains nearly 21 per cent oxygen. On the way out, this is down to 16 per cent; the extra 4 or 5 per cent is made up by carbon dioxide. Your breathing is controlled by your brain. When your muscles work harder they need more oxygen, which they take from your blood, and so the oxygen level of blood falls (and its carbon dioxide level rises). Your brain detects this and orders your breathing muscles to work harder and faster, to bring in more oxygen. When full, your lungs hold five or more litres of air. While you are resting or asleep, you take about one breath every three or four seconds. At the end of a race you could be "gasping for breath" twice a second, and taking in 15 times as much air as you did when resting.

Inside the lungs

The bigger the surface for absorbing oxygen, the more oxygen you can absorb. In each lung there are over 300 million tiny "air bubbles" called *alveoli*. If you spread the bubble walls out flat, they would cover a tennis court! So the lungs are well designed for their job. Hairs in the nose and the sticky linings of the air passages filter the air you breathe in, to clean it before it enters the lungs.

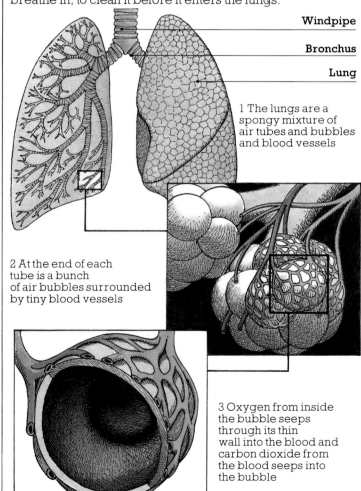

Windpipe

Bronchus

Lung

1 The lungs are a spongy mixture of air tubes and bubbles and blood vessels

2 At the end of each tube is a bunch of air bubbles surrounded by tiny blood vessels

3 Oxygen from inside the bubble seeps through its thin wall into the blood and carbon dioxide from the blood seeps into the bubble

As you breathe in

The sheet of muscle at the base of your chest is your diaphragm. When slack and relaxed, it forms a dome shape, and your lungs are small (as shown). To breathe in, it contracts and flattens. The muscles between your ribs also contract to pull the ribs up and out. These actions make your chest bigger and stretch the lungs inside. Air is sucked in through your mouth and down your windpipe.

The ins and outs of breathing

Your lungs (and your heart) fill your chest. Air tubes called bronchi *run up from them to the main air tube, your windpipe* (trachea), *which connects to your throat. Breathing in uses two main sets of muscles between the ribs and at the bottom of the chest. Breathing out happens automatically when you relax these muscles.*

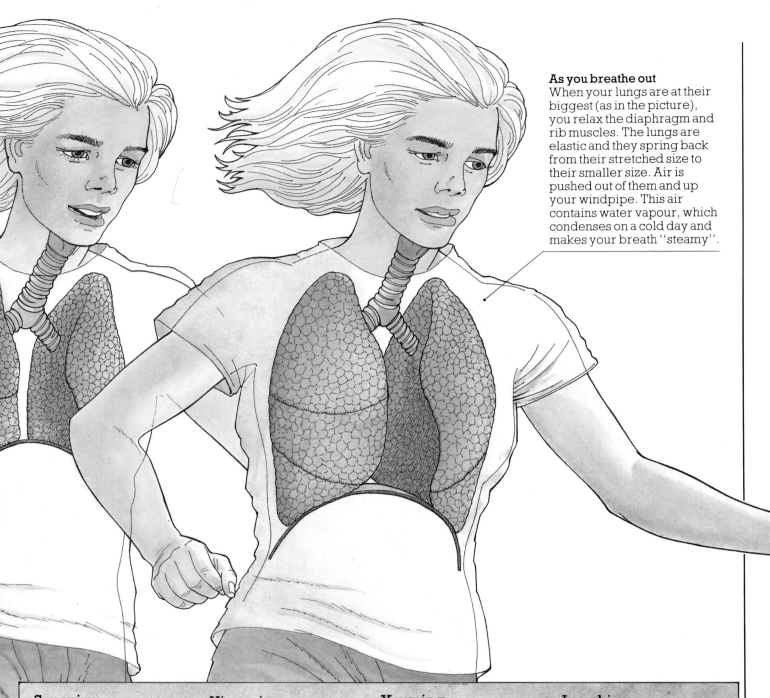

As you breathe out
When your lungs are at their biggest (as in the picture), you relax the diaphragm and rib muscles. The lungs are elastic and they spring back from their stretched size to their smaller size. Air is pushed out of them and up your windpipe. This air contains water vapour, which condenses on a cold day and makes your breath "steamy".

Sneezing

You close your throat while air pressure builds up in your lungs. Then you suddenly let the air go, and it blows out dust or germs from your nose.

Hiccuping

A hiccup is made by your diaphragm contracting more violently than it usually does. It can be caused by eating or drinking too quickly.

Yawning

You yawn when bored or tired. It may be that you are not breathing deeply enough and carbon dioxide has built up. A yawn might clear it.

Laughing

Laughter is several sudden jerks of the diaphragm which force air up the windpipe and through the voice box. Trying to stop can make it worse!

39

THE HEART

Blood is the body's transport system (*as explained on page 16*). At the centre of this system is your heart. It has four chambers with muscular walls. About once a second, the walls contract and squeeze blood out of the chambers into strong tubes, called arteries. The blood is pushed around your body. As the heart relaxes again, its chambers fill with more blood brought back to it by other tubes, the veins. This pumping, which we call a heart beat, happens every second of every day, for as long as you live. You can feel blood surging through the artery in your wrist. Each surge or "pulse" is one heart beat. So your "pulse rate" tells you how fast your heart is beating.

No man-made pump is as reliable as your heart. It can beat for 100 years or more without a rest. Also, the heart is adjustable. It can beat faster or slower, and change how much blood it pumps with each beat, depending on how active you are. The adjustments are controlled by nerves from your brain and by hormones. When you are resting your heart might beat 60 to 70 times a minute, and pump about 70 millilitres (one-eighth of a pint) of blood each time. When you run a race it beats over twice as fast and pumps three times as much blood with each beat.

The traffic junction
The heart is like a traffic junction. Arteries and veins lead in and out of it, taking blood to where it is needed. In fact, the heart is not one pump but two, side by side. The right side sends stale blood which has been round your body (the blue loads in the picture) to the lungs. There it collects fresh oxygen (the red loads). This blood then flows back to the left side of the heart, which pumps it all round your body. When it returns it has given up its oxygen (blue loads again) and flows back to the right side of the heart.

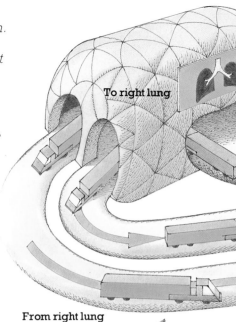

To right lung

From right lung

Back from the body
Stale blood flows from your body back to your heart along thin-walled, floppy tubes called veins. By the time blood has passed through all your tissues it no longer moves in powerful surges, as it does in the arteries, so the veins do not have to have strong walls. Some veins have one-way valves, to make sure blood keeps flowing in the right direction.

From body and legs

How the heart pumps

Each side of your heart has two chambers. The upper one (*atrium*) is small and has thin walls. It swells as blood flows into it. The blood then passes through a valve to the lower chamber (*ventricle*). This is bigger and has a thick, muscular wall. The left lower chamber provides the power to push blood all round your body, from your head to your toes. The right lower chamber is slightly smaller and sends blood to your lungs. (The labels seem the wrong way round because it's *your* right side, facing you.)

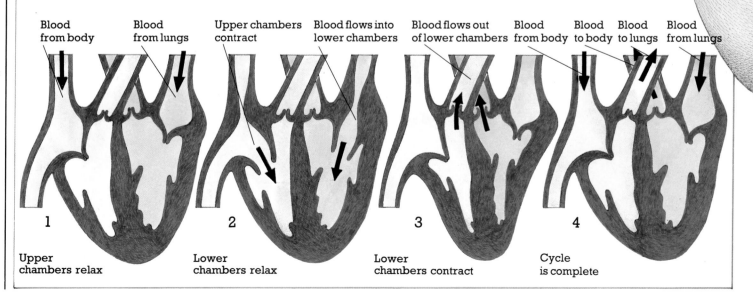

Blood from body   **Blood from lungs**   **Upper chambers contract**   **Blood flows into lower chambers**   **Blood flows out of lower chambers**   **Blood from body**   **Blood to body**   **Blood to lungs**   **Blood from lungs**

1 — Upper chambers relax

2 — Lower chambers relax

3 — Lower chambers contract

4 — Cycle is complete

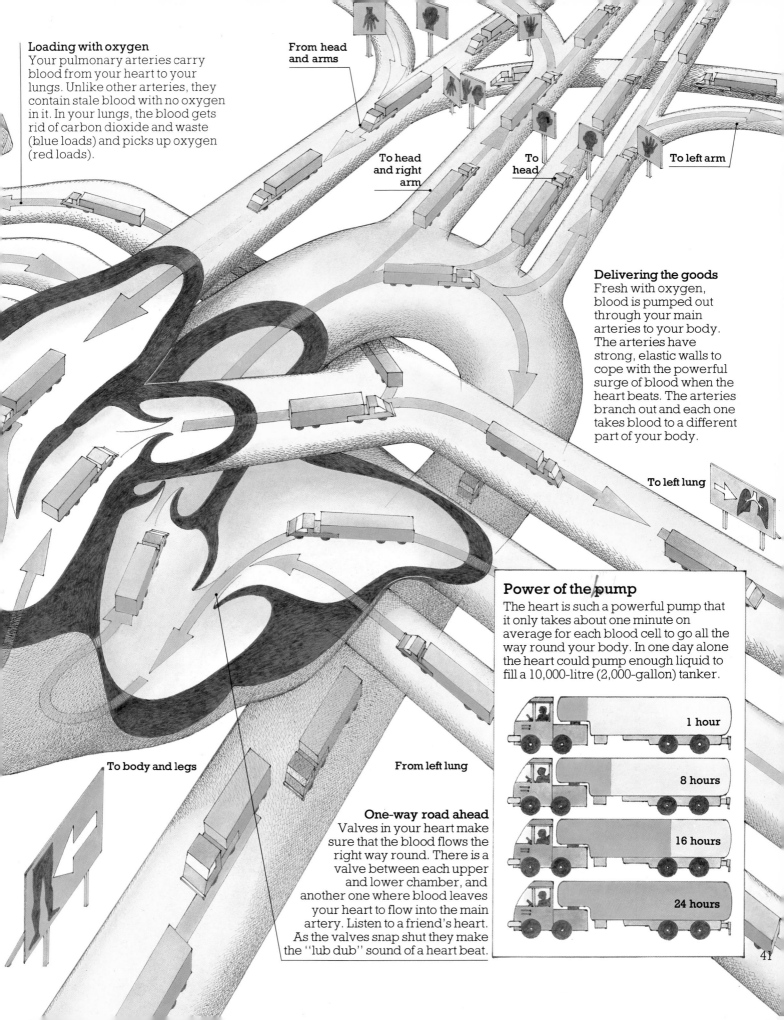

Loading with oxygen
Your pulmonary arteries carry blood from your heart to your lungs. Unlike other arteries, they contain stale blood with no oxygen in it. In your lungs, the blood gets rid of carbon dioxide and waste (blue loads) and picks up oxygen (red loads).

From head and arms

To head and right arm

To head

To left arm

Delivering the goods
Fresh with oxygen, blood is pumped out through your main arteries to your body. The arteries have strong, elastic walls to cope with the powerful surge of blood when the heart beats. The arteries branch out and each one takes blood to a different part of your body.

To left lung

Power of the pump
The heart is such a powerful pump that it only takes about one minute on average for each blood cell to go all the way round your body. In one day alone the heart could pump enough liquid to fill a 10,000-litre (2,000-gallon) tanker.

1 hour

8 hours

16 hours

24 hours

To body and legs

From left lung

One-way road ahead
Valves in your heart make sure that the blood flows the right way round. There is a valve between each upper and lower chamber, and another one where blood leaves your heart to flow into the main artery. Listen to a friend's heart. As the valves snap shut they make the "lub dub" sound of a heart beat.

41

ARMS AND HANDS

Look closely at your arms and hands. They are so well designed that they can do an enormous variety of jobs, from threading a needle to lifting a sack of potatoes. Besides moving and handling, they can feel. The skin on your fingertips is especially sensitive and can detect movements too small to see.

It is difficult for engineers to copy the design of the arm and hand for use in a machine. The computer-controlled "robot arms" in car factories are similar to our arms in some ways, but they are much simpler. They can only do a few tasks and they soon wear out. The human arm lasts for years and years. It rarely goes wrong and can mend itself when injured. And of course it is controlled by the most complicated computer of all – the human brain.

Why has the human body got hands and arms? Why aren't we four-legged, like dogs and cats and so many other animals? The reason is probably to do with feeding. Our monkey-like ancestors lived among the trees, using all four limbs to move about. But they also used their front limbs to pick fruits, shoots, leaves and flowers, to catch small animals, and to put these things into their mouths to eat. When the first humans began to walk on two legs, their arms were not needed to help them move about any more. Gradually these early people learned that they could pick up and fiddle with other things beside food. Pieces of stone, wood and bone could be made into tools. This was the beginning of our success. The human body has a clever brain, but it is the arms, hands and fingers that make it possible to carry out its ideas.

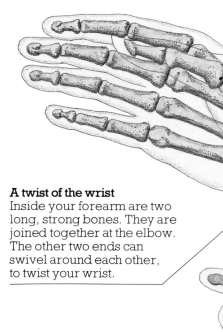

Thumbs up
Your thumb can swivel to touch each fingertip in turn. This enables you to pick up and hold things delicately and precisely.

A twist of the wrist
Inside your forearm are two long, strong bones. They are joined together at the elbow. The other two ends can swivel around each other, to twist your wrist.

Open and closed
There are 20 muscles in your hand itself. With the 14 muscles in your arm that connect to your hand, you can move your fingers into almost any position you wish.

Two levers for your hand
Under its skin, your arm is made mostly of muscles and bones. Your upper arm and forearm work like two adjustable levers, so that you can put your hand exactly where you want it. Your palm and fingers do the grasping, gripping and – just as important – the letting go.

Wrist bands
Just about where you wear a watch strap, there are ligaments – bands of tough, stringy tissue wrapped around your wrist to strengthen it. Under them slide long, thin tendons that work your fingers. There are over 20 tendons in each wrist.

Inside a fingertip
Imagine walking about with your eyes closed. You would probably hold your hands out in front of you so that your fingers could feel for anything in the way. The skin of your fingertips is packed with nerve endings that can detect the lightest touch (*see page 12*) as well as heat, cold and pain. The hard nail at the back of your fingertip gives the skin something solid to be squeezed against as you feel things. Without a nail, your whole fingertip would bend when you touched something and you would not be able to feel so well.

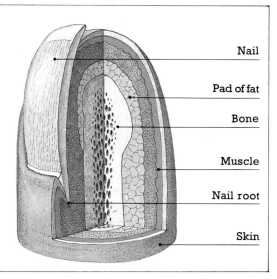

Nail

Pad of fat

Bone

Muscle

Nail root

Skin

Animal "nails"
Your nails are made of a tough substance that is similar to hardened skin. The claws, hooves and horns of other animals are made of the same substance, which is called *keratin*. Because we do not use our "claws" for tearing up food or fighting (not usually, anyway) they have become much smaller than the claws of many animals. Your nails grow about one millimetre in two weeks on average, and your finger nails grow slightly faster than your toe nails. Both your finger and toe nails grow more slowly in winter.

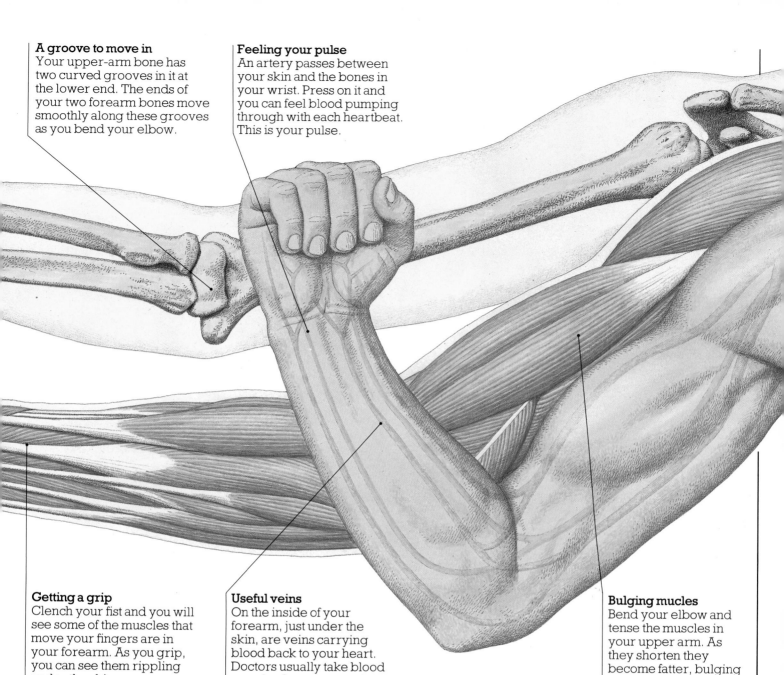

A groove to move in
Your upper-arm bone has two curved grooves in it at the lower end. The ends of your two forearm bones move smoothly along these grooves as you bend your elbow.

Feeling your pulse
An artery passes between your skin and the bones in your wrist. Press on it and you can feel blood pumping through with each heartbeat. This is your pulse.

Getting a grip
Clench your fist and you will see some of the muscles that move your fingers are in your forearm. As you grip, you can see them rippling under the skin.

Useful veins
On the inside of your forearm, just under the skin, are veins carrying blood back to your heart. Doctors usually take blood samples from these veins.

Bulging mucles
Bend your elbow and tense the muscles in your upper arm. As they shorten they become fatter, bulging under your skin.

The hawk's talons

A hawk uses its strong, sharp talons for seizing hold of its prey as it swoops, and for holding the prey still while it tears it apart with its sharp beak.

The bear's claws

Bears eat most kinds of food. They hunt for fish and small animals, and they dig for roots. Their claws are not particularly sharp, but they are strong.

The horse's hooves

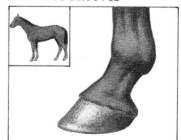

Most animals have five "claws" on each leg. A horse only has one. This is the hoof, which has become large and strong to support the horse's weight.

The goat's horns

Some animals have horns which are made from hardened skin with bone inside. The goat uses its horns to defend itself when it is frightened.

THE ABDOMEN

The lower half of your main body is called your abdomen. Inside it, many organs are squashed together. They are mainly to do with the "ins" and "outs" of food – taking new food into the body, and getting rid of the old food and other unwanted things. Most of the space is taken up by your intestines, the "in" organs. They digest food

The base of your back
The wedge-shaped bone at the bottom of your back is called the sacrum. It is made of five separate backbones that merge into one while you are a child.

Keep a straight back
Five backbones in your abdomen are large and strong, to carry the weight of your head, arms and body. If you bend badly here, you can get backache.

Long and thin
Packed into your abdomen, and filling most of its lower part, are the coils of your small intestine. Here digested food is absorbed into your blood stream.

Shorter and wider
Your large intestine is shorter than your small intestine, but much wider. It curls around your small intestine and absorbs spare water from left-over food.

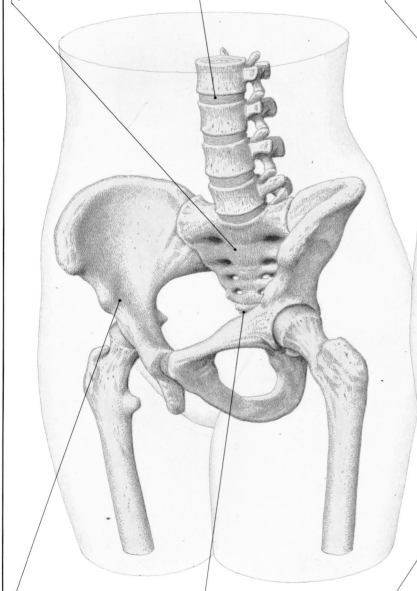

A bowl of bone
Your hip bone, made of several bones joined together, is shaped like a bowl. It helps to protect the soft organs in the lower part of your abdomen.

A strange "tail"
At the very base of your backbone is your "tail". It is made of three or four small backbones joined into one. In some animals these bones are much longer.

A new life
In a woman, the base of the abdomen contains the ovaries (which hold the eggs) and the womb, where a baby grows. In men, this place is filled with intestines.

Waste disposal
Your bladder stores urine from your kidneys. Behind it (in women) is the womb. As your bladder slowly fills with urine it squashes up your intestines.

and absorb it into your bloodstream, so that it can be carried around your body. They let any food that cannot be digested pass straight through. Your liver and kidneys are the main "out" organs. They filter blood and deal with the unwanted things it brings from other parts of the body. This keeps your blood clear of waste matter, which would build up and become poisonous if it was not removed. Although you cannot feel it or see anything from the outside, the organs in your abdomen rarely stay still. Your intestines, especially, squirm and squeeze as they push food along.

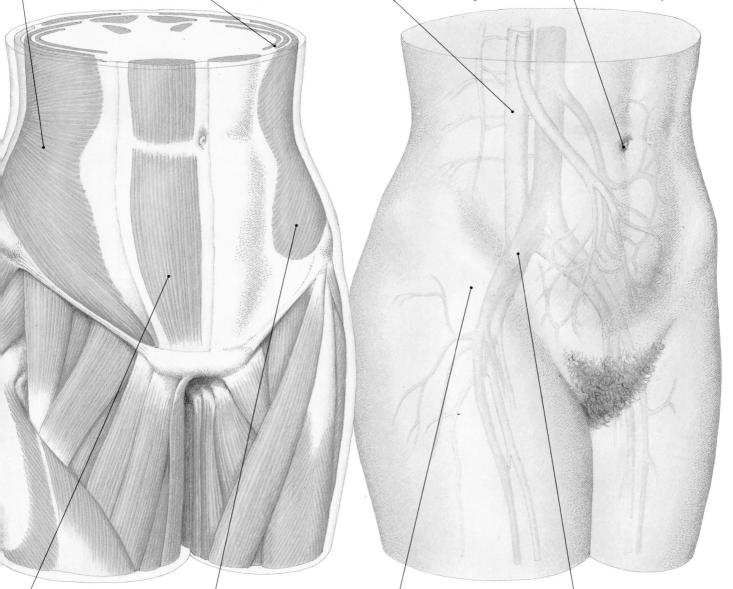

Four sheets of muscles
At the front, there are no bones to strengthen your abdomen. Instead there are four sets of muscles. Three of them are flat sheets; this one runs diagonally.

Muscles on your side
This layer of muscle is the innermost of the three sheets. It runs from your front around to your back, in part of your chest as well well as your abdomen.

An uphill struggle
Next to the artery is the main vein taking blood from your abdomen and legs back to your heart. As you walk, your leg muscles help to push blood up this vein.

Where the lifeline was
In the womb the umbilical cord was your "lifeline". After birth (*see pages 54-55*) it was cut and the end dropped off, leaving your navel or "belly button".

A strong strap
Inside the three sheets of muscle is this strap-shaped muscle. It runs from the front of your hip bone to your ribs. There is one on each side of your abdomen.

Criss-crossed for strength
The outer sheet of the three sheets of muscle runs diagonally. With the up-and-down and side-to-side sets of muscles, the front of the abdomen is very strong.

Fight the flab
In some people the skin over the abdomen is full of fat. The fat is a food store for times of need. Too much fat is unhealthy and means you eat too much.

Blood for the abdomen
The main artery from your heart runs down just inside your backbone. Branches of if fork off to your intestines, liver, kidneys and other abdominal organs.

WHERE YOUR FOOD GOES

You swallow some food, and for you it seems like the end of the matter. But for your food it is only the beginning. Ahead lies an amazing journey lasting perhaps two days, travelling through more than 8 metres (over 25 feet) of tubes, chambers and pipes. These make up your digestive system. The job of the digestive system is to take what you eat and break it down (*digest* it) into pieces tiny enough to be absorbed into your body.

The digestive system is basically one long tube, starting at the mouth and ending at the anus. But some parts of the tube are narrow, others are wide. Some parts of it are long and others are short. The shape of each part depends on what it does.

Swallowed food takes several seconds to go down your throat and then down a muscular tube which is called your gullet or *oesophagus*. It ends up in your stomach. Here it is crushed and squashed and mixed with digestive chemicals into a thick, creamy soup. From your stomach, the soupy food is squeezed slowly into your small intestine. Here, the useful bits of food pass through the lining of the tube and into your blood stream.

Meanwhile the leftover bits of food pass into a shorter, wider tube, your large intestine. In this, most of the water is absorbed from the leftovers and they become more solid. Finally they are stored at the end of your large intestine, until it's convenient to get rid of them.

Only some parts of your food are taken into your body. These useful bits are called *nutrients*. They will be used for body-building, growth and repair and to give you energy. The leftover parts of your food are not digested, but this does not mean they are useless. Some indigestible parts give your food "bulk". They help your digestive system to grip the food as it passes slowly through the tubes. This useful, but undigested, part of the food is called *fibre*.

When you swallow food it seems to go "into" your body. But this is not really true. The food goes into the tunnel that runs through your digestive system, like the hole in a pipe. But it cannot get into your organs and tissues until it is absorbed through the lining of the small intestine. Only then is the food truly inside your body.

The destruction line
In many factories, goods are put together piece by piece on a "production line". Your digestive system does the opposite. It pulls your food apart, bit by bit. So it is not a production line, it's a "destruction line". On the next four pages you can see a slightly untangled view of the stomach and other digestive organs, with a day's worth of meals passing through at various stages.

Pushing food along
Food doesn't just fall down into your stomach. The muscles in your gullet wall contract to make a sort of "travelling wave" that pushes the food in front of it. This is called *peristalsis*. It means you can swallow even when you are lying down! In fact food is pushed through your entire digestive system by peristalsis.

Dealing with nutrients
Your liver receives blood full of freshly-digested nutrients from your small intestine. The liver sorts out the nutrients. It stores some, changes some, and lets others pass through to other parts of the body.

Gullet

Liver

Four-in-one stomach
A cow's stomach has not got one chamber, like yours, but four chambers. Chewed grass goes first into the rumen, where it is partly digested. Later, the cow brings up this food and chews it some more ("chewing the cud"). Then it is swallowed again and goes into the other chambers. This double-digestion helps the cow to get maximum nourishment from its tough food of grasses and plants.

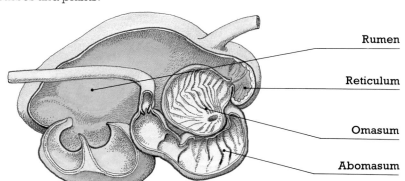

Rumen

Reticulum

Omasum

Abomasum

A bag for your lunch

Your packed lunch is in a box all morning and a bag all afternoon – your stomach. Strong muscles in the stomach wall crush the food to a pulp. Its lining makes acids and other chemicals that dissolve the food.

Chemical attack

Strong digestive juices are made in your pancreas, which is just under your stomach. They flow along a narrow tube into your duodenum where they attack the food chemically and dissolve it into tiny pieces.

What your body needs

Most foods are all right for you to eat – as long as you don't eat too much of any one thing. Your body needs regular supplies of a good variety of foods to stay healthy and keep working properly, as different types of food do different jobs. It needs protein for building new tissues, and carbohydrates and some fats for energy ... certain diseases, ... ing well. And water, in ... alive for a longer time

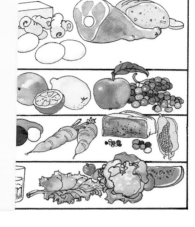

(handwritten note: Diagrahm of Stomach, shows whats inside of it.)

Dealing with fats

Fatty food is awkward to digest. The gall bladder stores bile, a digestive juice made by the liver. After a meal, bile flows down the bile duct into the duodenum. Here it begins to *emulsify* fats – break them down into tiny droplets which the other digestive juices can then attack more easily.

Gall bladder

Stomach

Pancreas

Small intestine

Large intestine

The beginning of the end

The first 25 centimetres (10 inches) or so of your small intestine is called the *duodenum*. Juices flow into it from your pancreas and gall bladder. It is the beginning of the end for the food you have eaten, which will soon be absorbed by the rest of your small intestine.

Pipes, tanks and chemicals

Like the pipes and tanks of a sewage farm, your digestive system is a series of tubes and chambers. Just as different chemicals are added to sewage at each stage, digestive juices are added to your food at different stages of its journey, to break it down. In both processes, waste is left over at the end.

The small intestine

This long tube snakes around your abdomen for 6 metres (20 feet) or so. It continually squeezes food along inside it, by peristalsis (see page 46).

Absorbing nutrients

In the lining of the small intestine there are many small blood vessels. Nutrients seep into the blood and are carried away, mainly to the liver.

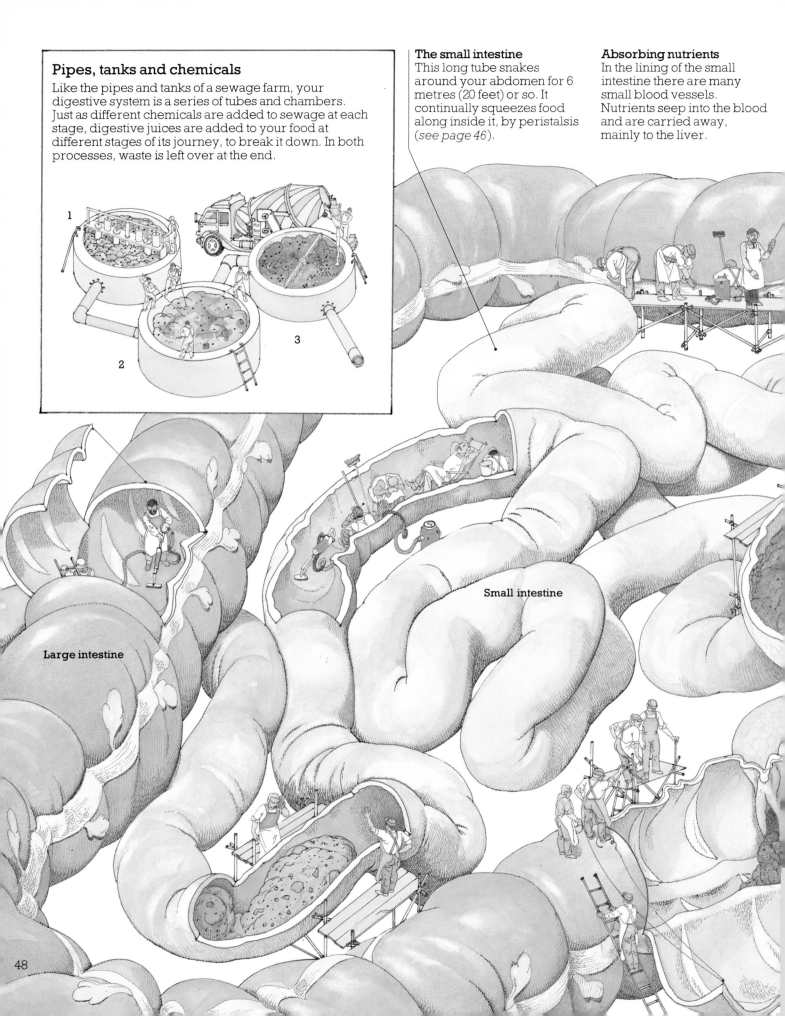

Large intestine

Small intestine

48

The large intestine

The "large" intestine is 1½ metres (5 feet) long, so it is much shorter than the "small" intestine. But it is three times as wide, at 7 centimetres (2½ inches).

Absorbing water

The watery leftovers in the large intestine become more solid as water is absorbed from them. Useful bacteria live here too, making some of the vitamins you need.

Inside the liver and kidneys

Your liver is in several parts, or *lobes*. It has a very rich blood flow. As well as dealing with the nutrients from digestion, it stores the energy-giving substances glucose and starch. It also stores vitamins, and breaks down old blood cells.

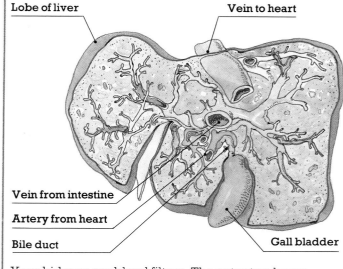

Lobe of liver

Vein to heart

Vein from intestine

Artery from heart

Bile duct

Gall bladder

Your kidneys are blood filters. The outer two layers filter waste chemicals from the blood. The waste trickles down microscopic tubes into the middle of the kidney, to form urine. This flows down a larger tube, the ureter, to the bladder.

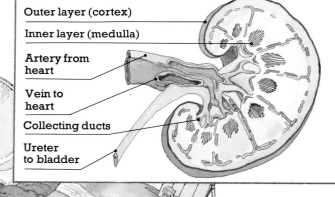

Outer layer (cortex)

Inner layer (medulla)

Artery from heart

Vein to heart

Collecting ducts

Ureter to bladder

Rectum

A useless organ

Where your small and large intestines join, is your appendix. This finger-like organ seems to have no use in the human body. But plant-eaters like rabbits have a much bigger appendix which helps them to digest tough plant food.

The end of the line

The "destruction line" has finished. Leftovers and waste wait to be removed in the *rectum*, the last part of the large intestine. The waste includes dead bacteria from the large intestine and rubbed-off bits of intestinal lining.

HOW YOU BEGAN

Every human being – and in fact every animal – begins life as one cell. This single cell contains all the instructions and information needed for a complete new animal to grow, develop and live its life. If all this information was written out in words it would fill many, many books. But the information is in the form of microscopic chemical codes, packed inside the single cell, which is smaller than a pinhead. This cell, the fertilized egg, is formed when a sperm cell from the father joins with an egg cell from the mother. At that moment, called *conception,* a new life begins.

How sperms are made

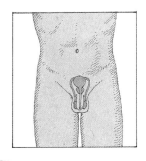

Sperms are made in a man's two *testes* (testicles). There is a continuous "production line" which makes 500 million new sperms each day. They are stored in the *epididymis,* a long coiled tube. If they are not needed to fertilize an egg, they die and are absorbed by the body.

Where eggs come from

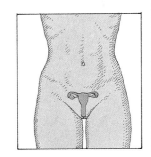

Eggs are stored in a woman's two ovaries. Each month an egg ripens and pops out of the ovary into the egg tube. The lining of the womb becomes thick with blood. If the egg is not fertilized, the lining comes away and passes out through the vagina. This is called *menstruation* or a "period".

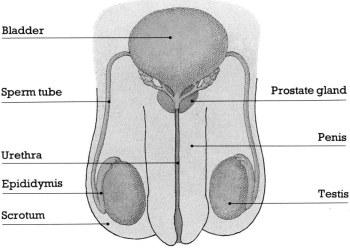

Bladder
Sperm tube
Prostate gland
Penis
Urethra
Epididymis
Scrotum
Testis

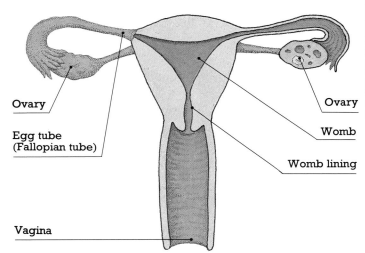

Ovary
Ovary
Egg tube (Fallopian tube)
Womb
Womb lining
Vagina

Making love

A baby starts to develop when a woman's egg cell and a man's sperm cell join together after the man and woman have had sexual intercourse or "made love". As the couple kiss and caress each other, they become sexually excited. The man's penis becomes larger and stiff or "erect" and the woman's vagina becomes firmer. The man slides his penis into the woman's vagina and at the climax of intercourse the muscles around his urethra contract, squirting about 300 million sperm, in a milky liquid called semen, out of the penis and into the woman's vagina. Like tadpoles, sperm have long tails to help them swim. They find the entrance to the womb and swim up through it into the egg tubes. The egg cell gives off a chemical which works a bit like a homing device, helping the sperm to find the way. Once the surviving sperm reach the egg, each of them tries to be the one to penetrate its outer membrane and fertilize it.

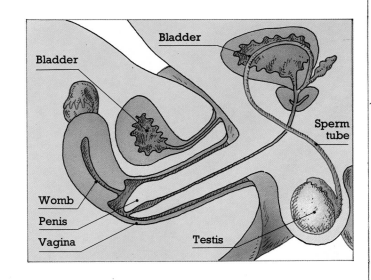

Bladder
Bladder
Sperm tube
Womb
Penis
Vagina
Testis

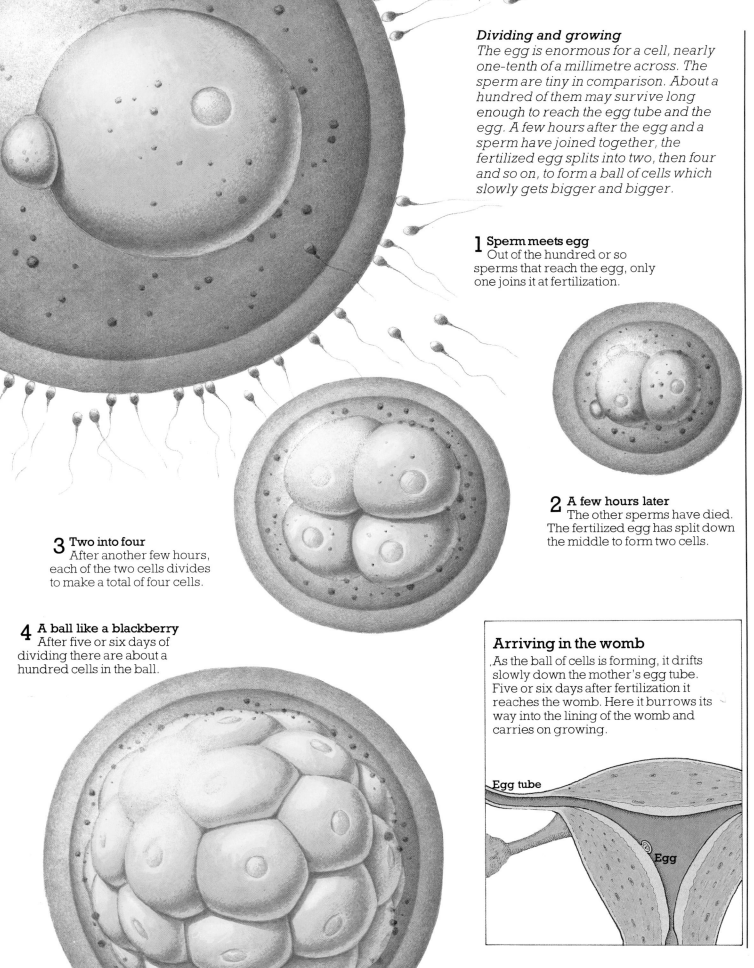

Dividing and growing

The egg is enormous for a cell, nearly one-tenth of a millimetre across. The sperm are tiny in comparison. About a hundred of them may survive long enough to reach the egg tube and the egg. A few hours after the egg and a sperm have joined together, the fertilized egg splits into two, then four and so on, to form a ball of cells which slowly gets bigger and bigger.

1 Sperm meets egg
Out of the hundred or so sperms that reach the egg, only one joins it at fertilization.

2 A few hours later
The other sperms have died. The fertilized egg has split down the middle to form two cells.

3 Two into four
After another few hours, each of the two cells divides to make a total of four cells.

4 A ball like a blackberry
After five or six days of dividing there are about a hundred cells in the ball.

Arriving in the womb

,As the ball of cells is forming, it drifts slowly down the mother's egg tube. Five or six days after fertilization it reaches the womb. Here it burrows its way into the lining of the womb and carries on growing.

Egg tube

Egg

BEFORE YOU WERE BORN

At the very beginning of your life you lived in your mother's womb. At first you were as small as a tiny dot, but your body grew and changed so much that after nine months of being in the womb you were ready to live in the outside world.

All the time you were in the womb, you lived inside a warm, safe bag full of watery liquid. You didn't eat through your mouth or breathe through your nose. You got all the air and food you needed from your mother's blood by means of a special tube attached at one end to your mother and at the other end to your tummy (*see page 54*).

After about three months in the womb you were able to move about, suck your thumb, and even turn somersaults. You slept a lot of the time, but when you were awake you could hear your mother's voice, the thumping of her heart, and the sound of food passing through her body.

After about nine months you were ready to be born.

The first nine months
Although you started life looking no bigger than a small dot, you soon began to look like a proper baby. During the time you were in your mother's womb, you practised a number of things that would help you after you were born. The most important things you practised were sucking and swallowing. This meant you could take milk from your mother's breast or from a baby's bottle as soon as you were born. You also learnt to grip with your fingers, cough, sneeze, yawn, hiccup and stretch.

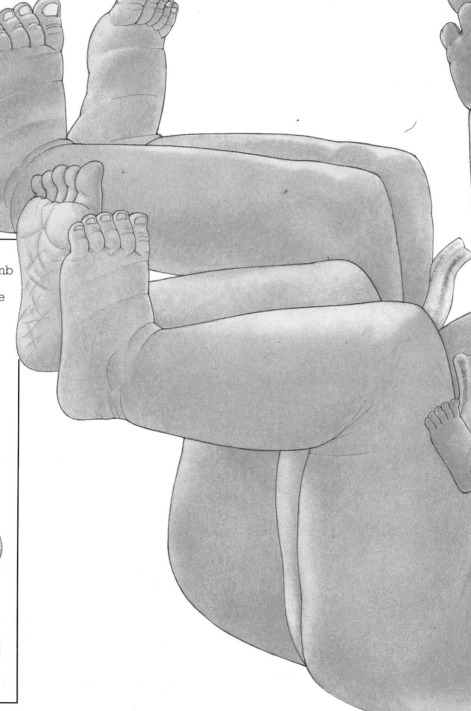

Whose baby?
At the very beginning of your life in the womb you looked like other baby animals. It was several weeks before you began to look like a human baby.

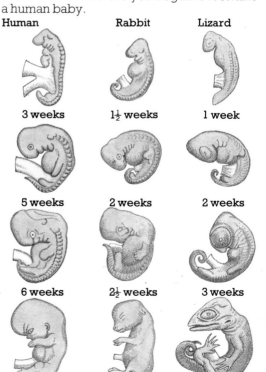

Human	Rabbit	Lizard
3 weeks	1½ weeks	1 week
5 weeks	2 weeks	2 weeks
6 weeks	2½ weeks	3 weeks
8 weeks	3 weeks	4 weeks

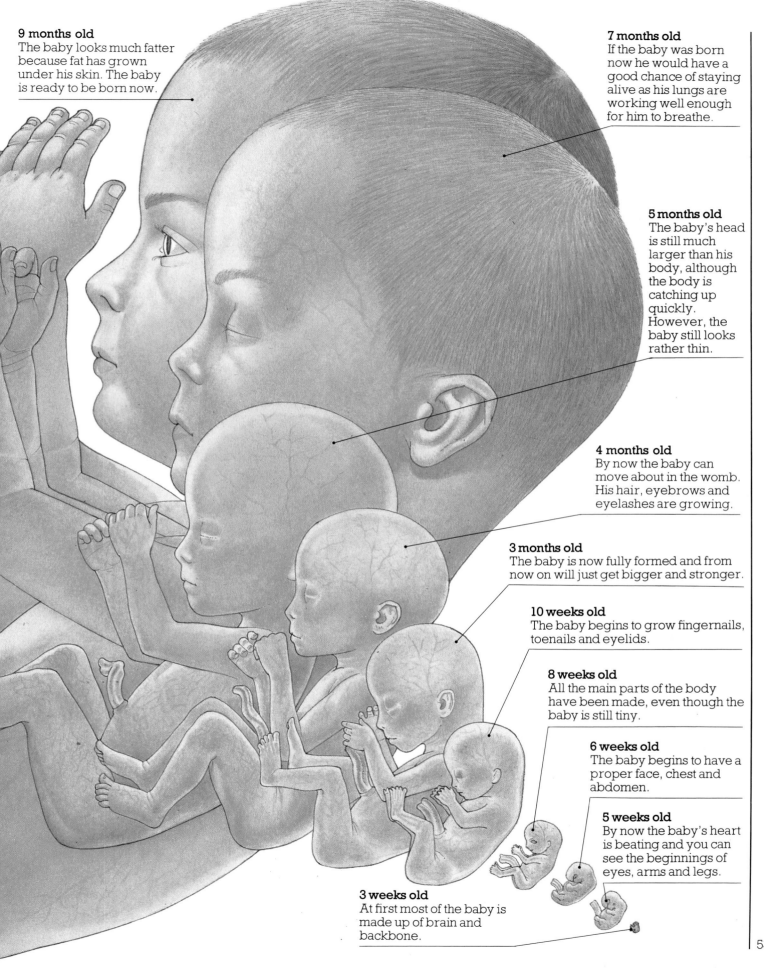

9 months old
The baby looks much fatter because fat has grown under his skin. The baby is ready to be born now.

7 months old
If the baby was born now he would have a good chance of staying alive as his lungs are working well enough for him to breathe.

5 months old
The baby's head is still much larger than his body, although the body is catching up quickly. However, the baby still looks rather thin.

4 months old
By now the baby can move about in the womb. His hair, eyebrows and eyelashes are growing.

3 months old
The baby is now fully formed and from now on will just get bigger and stronger.

10 weeks old
The baby begins to grow fingernails, toenails and eyelids.

8 weeks old
All the main parts of the body have been made, even though the baby is still tiny.

6 weeks old
The baby begins to have a proper face, chest and abdomen.

5 weeks old
By now the baby's heart is beating and you can see the beginnings of eyes, arms and legs.

3 weeks old
At first most of the baby is made up of brain and backbone.

YOUR FIRST JOURNEY

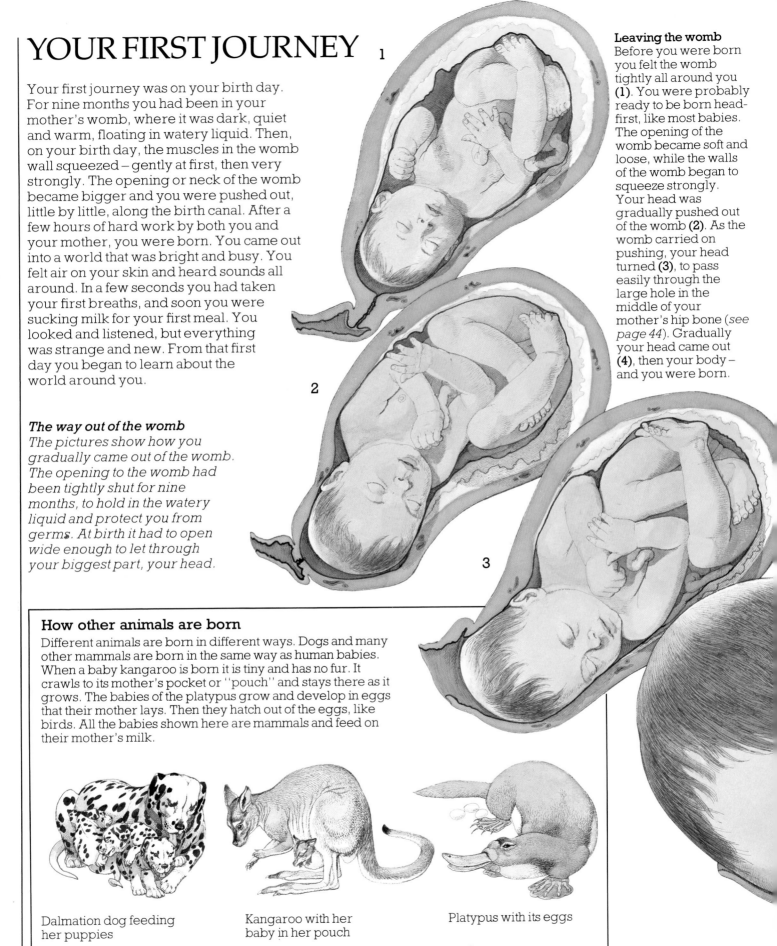

Your first journey was on your birth day. For nine months you had been in your mother's womb, where it was dark, quiet and warm, floating in watery liquid. Then, on your birth day, the muscles in the womb wall squeezed – gently at first, then very strongly. The opening or neck of the womb became bigger and you were pushed out, little by little, along the birth canal. After a few hours of hard work by both you and your mother, you were born. You came out into a world that was bright and busy. You felt air on your skin and heard sounds all around. In a few seconds you had taken your first breaths, and soon you were sucking milk for your first meal. You looked and listened, but everything was strange and new. From that first day you began to learn about the world around you.

The way out of the womb

The pictures show how you gradually came out of the womb. The opening to the womb had been tightly shut for nine months, to hold in the watery liquid and protect you from germs. At birth it had to open wide enough to let through your biggest part, your head.

Leaving the womb

Before you were born you felt the womb tightly all around you **(1)**. You were probably ready to be born head-first, like most babies. The opening of the womb became soft and loose, while the walls of the womb began to squeeze strongly. Your head was gradually pushed out of the womb **(2)**. As the womb carried on pushing, your head turned **(3)**, to pass easily through the large hole in the middle of your mother's hip bone (*see page 44*). Gradually your head came out **(4)**, then your body – and you were born.

How other animals are born

Different animals are born in different ways. Dogs and many other mammals are born in the same way as human babies. When a baby kangaroo is born it is tiny and has no fur. It crawls to its mother's pocket or "pouch" and stays there as it grows. The babies of the platypus grow and develop in eggs that their mother lays. Then they hatch out of the eggs, like birds. All the babies shown here are mammals and feed on their mother's milk.

Dalmation dog feeding her puppies

Kangaroo with her baby in her pouch

Platypus with its eggs

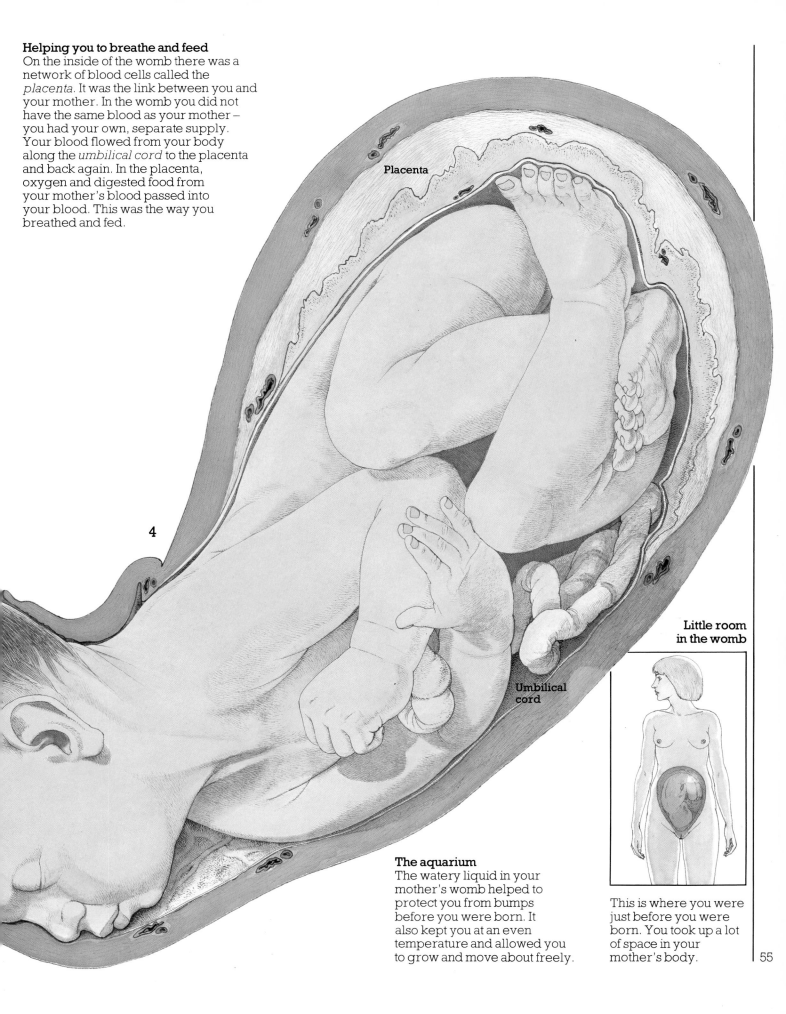

Helping you to breathe and feed
On the inside of the womb there was a network of blood cells called the *placenta*. It was the link between you and your mother. In the womb you did not have the same blood as your mother – you had your own, separate supply. Your blood flowed from your body along the *umbilical cord* to the placenta and back again. In the placenta, oxygen and digested food from your mother's blood passed into your blood. This was the way you breathed and fed.

Placenta

Umbilical cord

Little room in the womb

The aquarium
The watery liquid in your mother's womb helped to protect you from bumps before you were born. It also kept you at an even temperature and allowed you to grow and move about freely.

This is where you were just before you were born. You took up a lot of space in your mother's body.

55

PARENT TO CHILD

Do you look like your mother or your father – or both? Most children look like their parents. You might have "your mother's eyes" or "your father's nose". Your parents, in turn, look similar to their parents, and your children will resemble you. The passing of family likeness from parents to children is called *heredity*. Yet no two people look exactly the same, unless they are "identical twins". Each of us is different. Why is this?

A baby grows from a fertilized egg, which contains all the instructions needed for a new human being to live and grow (*see page 50*). The instructions are called *genes* and there are many thousands of them. They control much of what a person looks like – the colour of his hair, skin and eyes, the shape of his nose and other facial features, and so on. Often many genes combine to determine a feature. There are two sets of genes. One set is *inherited* from the mother, in the egg, and the other set comes from the father, in the sperm. As a new baby grows, the mother's genes control some features while the father's genes are in charge of others. If a feature is controlled by many genes, they can form different combinations of the mother's and father's genes.

The "mixing and matching" of genes happens quite by chance. It explains why you look similar to your parents, but not exactly the same as them.

From grandparent to grandchild
Can you see the similarities between these people? The two below are grandparents. The woman to the right is their daughter and her husband is next to her. The two youngest ones are the grandchildren.

Fair or red?
Hair colour can change through life. Some people dye their hair. In others it is lightened by the sun, or it goes grey with age (especially in men). But hair's natural colour is controlled by genes inherited from mother and father.

The grandmother below has passed her fair hair on to the mother. The father has brought red hair into the family. Their son has inherited red hair from his father, while the daughter has inherited her fair hair from her mother.

Boy or girl?

Whether you are a boy or girl depends on genes. These are found on tiny *chromosomes*. There are 23 chromosomes in an egg and 23 in each sperm. One of the 23 is the sex chromosome. The egg's sex chromosome is always X. The sperm's can be X or Y. When an X-carrying sperm joins an egg, the fertilized egg has two X chromosomes. XX is the code for a girl. With a Y-carrying sperm, the result is XY, the code for a boy. On average half the sperm carry an X chromosome and half a Y chromosome, so half the children born are girls and the other half boys.

Father XY   Mother XX

Sperm   Sperm   Egg   Egg

X   Y   X   X

Girl XX   Boy XY   Girl XX   Boy XY

Family groups

Humans are like one big family. Apart from different shades of skin, hair and eyes, and being tall or short, we all look basically the same. All the people in the world belong to the same group, or *species*. It's the same for other animals. All horses look much the same, and belong to the horse species. Zebras form a species of their own.

Blue or brown?

Eye colour is passed from parent to child. Like other features, there are two genes controlling it – one from the mother and one from the father. But in this case the two genes are not the same strength.

A "brown" gene, giving brown eyes, is stronger than a "blue" gene. In the family below, each grandparent has blue eyes, so each of them must have two "blue" genes. The mother has inherited "blue" genes, so

she has blue eyes. The father has "blue" and "brown" genes, and his eyes are brown. Their son has two "blue" genes, but their daughter has brown eyes as she has inherited her father's "brown" genes.

It runs in the family

The son in the picture below has inherited his "grandmother's nose". This means that his nose is the same shape as hers. He can pass the genes which determine this nose on to future generations.

THE CHANGING BODY

Throughout life, the human body changes in size and shape. It starts as a tiny speck called a fertilized egg. In nine months this grows into a baby, ready to be born (*see page 51*). After birth we can see the changes as a baby grows. To begin with, these happen very quickly. During childhood the body is still growing, but the speed of growth gradually slows down. As a person reaches adulthood, at about 20 years of age, growth stops.

No one understands how the body "knows" when to stop growing. It may be that some cells in the body have "clocks" in them that count the number of times they divide. (More cells means a bigger body.) When the number of divisions reaches a certain amount, the cells stop dividing, and so growth stops.

Between about 20 and 50 years of age, the body does not change much in outward appearance. Yet there is always activity inside. Nutrients in food are used to build new tissues to replace worn-out ones. Then, as old age approaches, the body cannot repair the wear and tear so quickly. Parts may start to go wrong, and people are more likely to fall ill. Even so, people who take care of their bodies when they are young can stay healthy well into old age.

Chemicals in control

Going round and round your body, in your blood, are chemicals called *hormones*. There are over 20 different hormones, and each one controls a particular body process. Some of these take years, such as growing up. Others go on all the time, such as adjusting the amounts of water and salt in your body.

Hormones are made in special glands called endocrine glands. Your adrenal glands, lying on top of your kidneys, make the hormone adrenaline. When you get excited or frightened the adrenal glands release adrenaline into your blood stream. Adrenaline affects many body organs. It makes your heart beat faster, your skin go sweaty and your lungs breathe more quickly, preparing your body for action.

Sex hormones from the ovaries control the cycle of egg release in women. In men, sex hormones from the testes control sperm production. Insulin, a hormone from the pancreas, controls the amount of sugar in your blood.

From small to tall

As a person grows, not all the parts of his body grow bigger at the same rate. A baby has a large head and body in proportion to his short arms and legs. Over the years his head grows only a little. His body grows slightly faster. His arms grow even faster, and his legs grow fastest of all. By the time he is grown up, his head and body are quite small in proportion to his arms and legs, which are long.

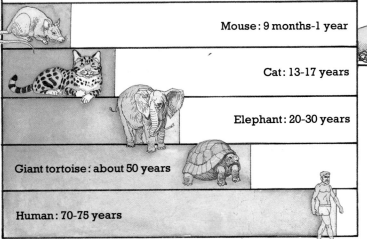

Who lives longest?

Compared to most other animals, humans have a long life. In general, the bigger an animal is, the longer it lives, as you can see below. Small creatures like insects, spiders and snails live only a few years on average. Some of the animals who live the longest are large reptiles like giant tortoises and crocodiles.

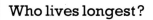

Mouse: 9 months-1 year

Cat: 13-17 years

Elephant: 20-30 years

Giant tortoise: about 50 years

Human: 70-75 years

1 year old
At this age, most babies are just beginning to learn to walk. The average baby is around 75 centimetres tall and weighs about 10 kilograms. Boys are often slightly taller and heavier than girls. A baby does not have to be chubby to be healthy, as some people think.

6 years old
The average six-year-old is nearly 120 centimetres tall and weighs almost 25 kilograms. He grows 5 centimetres taller and 2½ kilograms heavier each year. His arms and legs are growing longer, and he has learned to walk, talk, run, throw, read and write.

14 years old
This is the time of puberty, when many changes occur all over the body. Boys have suddenly started growing more quickly – eight centimetres a year for three years or so. Girls do the same, but their growth spurt starts when they are about eleven or twelve.

20 years
Most people are fully grown by this age, at least in their height. Men average 174 centimetres tall and women 161 centimetres. Weight tends to vary much more, depending on how much you eat! The muscles have not yet reached their full development.

45-50 years old
During middle age there are few outward changes in the body. Some people, especially men, may put on a little weight. Some men also start to lose hair from the top of the head. A few wrinkles may appear in the skin, especially for people living in sunny places.

60-70 years old
The skin gradually becomes more wrinkled. And most people become shorter, so they are five to seven centimetres smaller than they were at the age of 20. This is because the discs between the backbones shrink, as do the muscles that help us stand upright.

LEGS AND FEET

Your arms and your legs are built from the same basic parts (*see page 19*). There are about the same number of bones and muscles in each. Your thigh, like your upper arm, has one long bone. Your calf, like your forearm, has two long bones. Your knee joint is similar to your elbow joint. But there are many small differences in the sizes and shapes of the parts. These add up to make your legs longer, stronger and less flexible than your arms. While arms are more suited to reaching and holding, legs are designed to carry the weight of your body and let you walk, run and jump. Your leg muscles are among the biggest and strongest in your body. When you run, they need lots of oxygen and energy, so you have to breathe faster and deeper, and your heart works harder to pump more blood to them.

Levers for walking

Like your arm, your leg is a double lever. In fact your foot acts as a short third lever, as you bend your ankle and push against the ground with the ball of your foot and toes when you walk or run. Inside, your leg is mostly bones and muscles.

Longest and strongest
Your thigh bone is the longest and strongest bone in your body. At the top its ball-shaped end fits snugly into a socket in your hip bone. Five strong straps called ligaments hold your hip and thigh bones together. Your hip joint is very strong, but it cannot move as freely as your shoulder joint.

Your largest joint
Your knee is the largest joint in your body. It is protected at the front by a small triangular bone, your knee cap. Your knees ''lock'' firmly when you stand with your legs straight. This means you use less muscle power, so standing is not too tiring.

The elastic foot
Like your wrist and hand, your ankle and foot are made of many bones – 26 in all. The foot bones form an elastic arch that flattens when you put your foot down and springs back to a curved shape when you lift it.

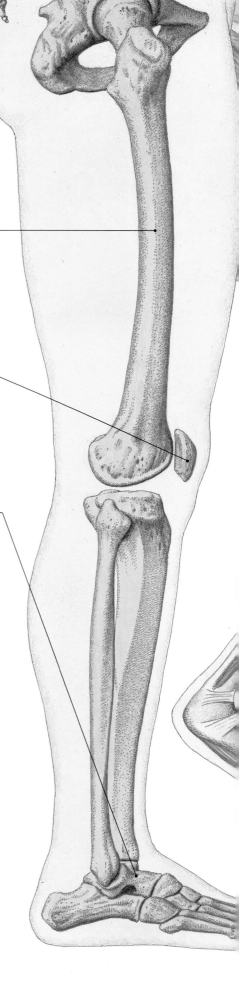

Jumping with joints

Each joint in your leg is different. Your hip is a *ball-and-socket* joint. It can move in any direction, like the ball-and-socket joint at the bottom of a computer joystick. Your knee is a *hinge* joint, like the hinge on a door. It can swing forwards and backwards, but not sideways. Your ankle is a *sliding* joint. Each ankle bone only moves a little, but the whole ankle is quite flexible. In general, the more directions a joint can move in, the weaker it is. Less movement means more strength. The knee is extremely strong but not very flexible. The shoulder is very flexible but not particularly strong, and sometimes the bones slip or ''dislocate''.

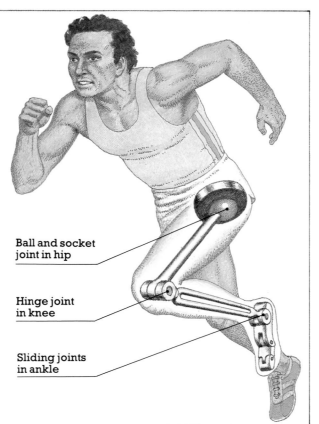

Ball and socket joint in hip

Hinge joint in knee

Sliding joints in ankle

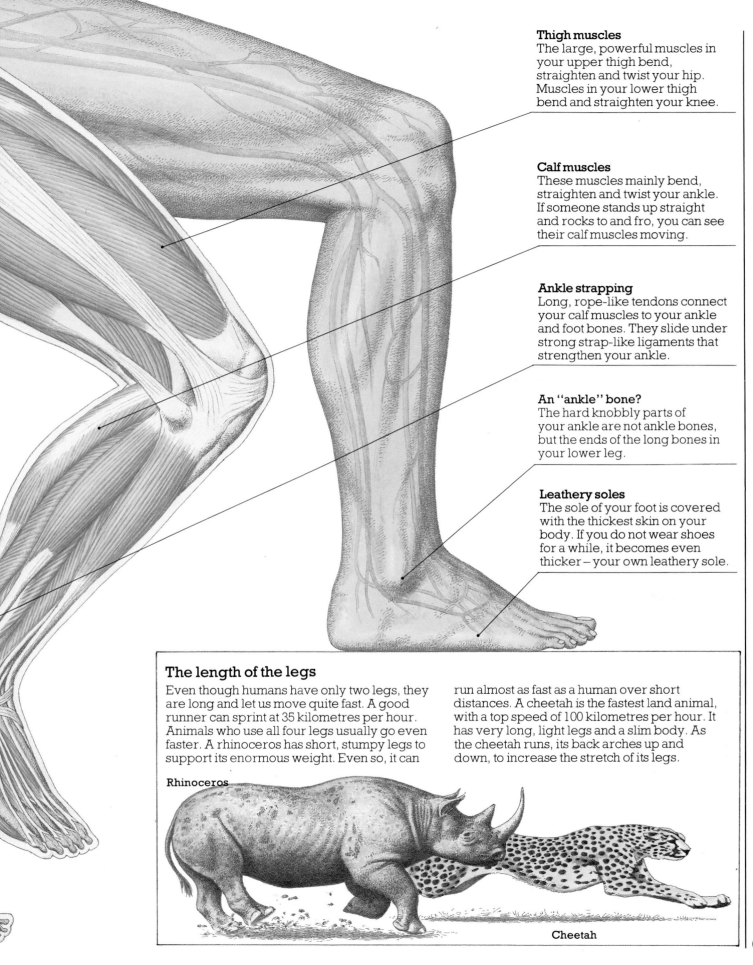

Thigh muscles
The large, powerful muscles in your upper thigh bend, straighten and twist your hip. Muscles in your lower thigh bend and straighten your knee.

Calf muscles
These muscles mainly bend, straighten and twist your ankle. If someone stands up straight and rocks to and fro, you can see their calf muscles moving.

Ankle strapping
Long, rope-like tendons connect your calf muscles to your ankle and foot bones. They slide under strong strap-like ligaments that strengthen your ankle.

An "ankle" bone?
The hard knobbly parts of your ankle are not ankle bones, but the ends of the long bones in your lower leg.

Leathery soles
The sole of your foot is covered with the thickest skin on your body. If you do not wear shoes for a while, it becomes even thicker – your own leathery sole.

The length of the legs

Even though humans have only two legs, they are long and let us move quite fast. A good runner can sprint at 35 kilometres per hour. Animals who use all four legs usually go even faster. A rhinoceros has short, stumpy legs to support its enormous weight. Even so, it can run almost as fast as a human over short distances. A cheetah is the fastest land animal, with a top speed of 100 kilometres per hour. It has very long, light legs and a slim body. As the cheetah runs, its back arches up and down, to increase the stretch of its legs.

Rhinoceros

Cheetah

GLOSSARY

The words in italics have their own entries in the glossary.

alveoli (singular: **alveolus**)
The tiny "bubbles" inside your lungs that fill with air as you breathe in.

atrium (plural: **atria**)
The upper chamber on each side of your heart.

bronchi (singular: **bronchus**)
The air tubes that join your lungs and the main air tube, your *trachea*.

capillaries
The microscopic tubes that carry blood to every *cell* of your body.

cells
The tiny living units that your body is made of.

cerebral cortexes
The two main areas of your brain.

chromosomes
The thread-like parts inside the nucleus of each *cell* that carry the genes.

cochlea
A snail-shaped tube that forms part of your inner ear.

cornea
The transparent area at the front of your eye.

cranium
The upper part of your skull.

dendrites
The "fingers" of your nerve cells, along which each *cell* can send signals to other nerve cells.

dermis
The lower layer of your skin, immediately beneath the *epidermis*.

diaphragm
The dome-shaped muscle, used in breathing, just beneath your lungs.

duodenum
The first part of your small intestine, where digestive juices dissolve food into tiny pieces.

epidermis
The outer layer of your skin.

Eustachian tube
The narrow tube joining the ear to the back of your throat.

Fallopian tubes
The two tubes joining a woman's ovaries to her womb.

follicles
Deep pits in your skin, from which hairs grow.

genes
The coded instructions, inherited from your parents, that determine your looks and characteristics.

heredity
The passing on of family likeness and characteristics through coded instructions called *genes*.

hormones
Chemicals that control your body's growth and development.

iris
The coloured part of your eye.

keratin
The hard substance that fingernails, claws, horns and hooves are made of.

lens
The area at the front of your eye, that focuses light rays onto the *retina*.

ligaments
Strong, strap-like fibres that hold your bones together.

marrow
The jelly-like substance inside your bones that makes all of your red blood cells and some of your white blood cells.

melanin
The colouring substance found in skin, that can darken it and protect it from damage by too much sun.

motor nerves
The nerves that carry instructions from the brain to the muscles.

myelin sheath
The fatty covering of the nerve fibre, along which signals are passed.

neurons
Another name for nerve cells.

oesophagus
Your gullet; the muscular tube joining the back of your throat to your stomach.

periosteum
The living "outer skin" or layer of your bones.

peristalsis
The "travelling wave", or muscular action, that pushes food down your gullet and through your entire digestive system.

plasma
The watery liquid that carries your blood cells and contains dissolved chemicals, such as salts.

platelets
Tiny fragments of cells in your blood that help it to clot.

puberty
A period of growth and sexual development during a person's teens.

rectum
The last part of your large intestine, in which waste is stored before it leaves your body.

reflex
An involuntary movement made by one of your muscles.

retina
The innermost layer of tissue at the back of your eyeball.

sacrum
The wedge-shaped bone at the bottom of your backbone.

sebaceous glands
Tiny glands in your skin that make "natural oils" to prevent it from drying out and cracking.

sensory nerves
The nerves that carry information from your sense organs to your brain.

tendons
The fibres that hold your muscles to your bones.

thalamus
The part of your brain that sorts out signals from your sense organs and redirects them to the appropriate area of the brain.

trachea
Your windpipe; the main air tube that connects your lungs to your throat.

ventricle
The lower chamber on each side of your heart.

vertebrae (singular: **vertebra**)
The separate bones of your backbone.

INDEX

The page numbers in bold type refer to major entries.

INDEX